LUSCIOUS chocolate DESSERTS

LUSCIOUS chocolate DESSERTS

by LORI LONGBOTHAM

PHOTOGRAPHS BY WILLIAM MEPPEM

CHRONICLE BOOKS

SAN FRANCISCO

ACKNOWLEDGMENTS

Thanks again to ANGELA MILLER, BILL LEBLOND, and AMY TREADWELL for making it happen and for making it fun. And to HOLLY BURROWS.

Special thanks to JUDITH SUTTON— I can't thank you enough, and for so many things. And many thanks to my usual favorite cast of characters— STEVE, LIZ, and SARAH LONGBOTHAM; AUNTIE JEAN; all the PERRYS; DEBORAH MINTCHEFF; ROSIE and SPROCKET; BARBARA OTTENHOFF; BARBARA HOWE; MARIE REGUSIS; SARAH MAHONEY; JEAN GALTON; SABRA TURNBULL; SHARON BOWERS; VALERIE CIPOLLONE; CAROL KRAMER; LISA TROLAND; TRACEY SEAMAN; SUSAN WESTMORELAND; DEBBY GOLDSMITH; CATHY LO; ROSANNE TOROIAN; DAVID BAILEY; SUSIE QUICK; JENA MYERS and her parents; SCOTT SMILEY; AND JENNIFER WEHRLE. More thanks to MARTHA HOLMBERG, AMY ALBERT, CAROL SPIER, LEIGH WOOD, JOANNA TORREY, JACK and JIM upstairs, NANCY ARUM, JOHN SCHARFFEN BERGER, ROBERT STEINBERG, DEBORAH KWAN, and BETH SHEPARD. And, of course, to JERRY.

DEDICATION For Mom, the sweetest

LIBRARY OF CONGRESS CATALOGING-IN-PUBLICATION DATA AVAILABLE.

ISBN 0-8118-3516-2

Manufactured in China

DESIGN BY JULIA FLAGG
PROP STYLING BY EMMA ROSS
FOOD STYLING BY SUSIE THEODOROU

Distributed in Canada by Raincoast Books
9050 Shaughnessy Street
Vancouver, British Columbia V6P 6E5

10 9 8 7 6 5 4 3

Chronicle Books LLC
85 Second Street
San Francisco, California 94105

www.chroniclebooks.com

When working with chocolate always wear brown.

—JUDITH OLNEY, *The Joy of Chocolate*

contents

INTRODUCTION

I AM
A
chocoholic.

Still.

Even after the more than **SIXTY POUNDS** of chocolate I used to develop the recipes for this book. **I love chocolate.** I have always loved chocolate. To paraphrase the supremely talented Sandra Boynton, also passionate about chocolate, **I am a person who likes chocolate,** as in I am a person who likes to breathe. At any given moment, I can tell you the last time I had chocolate and can anticipate (within three seconds) the next time I will have chocolate.

When I reflect on my life, I don't remember events and feelings in the context of which year they happened. No, when my life flashes in front of me, passages are marked by the chocolate desserts I was obsessed with at the time. In my youth, it was FROZEN CHOCOLATE-DIPPED BANANAS on the boardwalk in Santa Cruz; HERSHEY BARS anytime and everywhere; and a BANANA IN THE SKIN, SPLIT AND STUFFED WITH CHOCOLATE CHIPS, WRAPPED IN FOIL, AND TOSSED INTO THE CAMPFIRE AT SUMMER CAMP. In grade school, my best friend's mom made what she called "spoon candy" on rainy days. It was like warm fudge, served in the saucepan and eaten with a spoon. I thought it was genius then and still do.

When I was a little older and started to cook, like many of us, it was all chocolate all the time. CHOCOLATE CHIP COOKIES (mine were the size of a small pizza), BROWNIES (both with and without nuts), FUDGE, and CHOCOLATE-COATED English toffee. In college, I met the simple and sublime "Chocolate Decadence" at Narsai's restaurant in Kensington, north of Berkeley. It's a dessert I will never forget—perfectly simple, with a completely intense flavor, it rocked my world. I had no idea there could be so much chocolate in one dessert. After graduating from the CULINARY INSTITUTE OF AMERICA, I moved to Manhattan and began my chocolate exploration of the city. I was immediately mesmerized by the TRUFFLES and the CHOCOLATE-DIPPED STRAWBERRIES at the local chocolate shop, the luscious cookies called "Chocolate Globs" at the SOHO CHARCUTERIE, and the Rigo Jansci (rich chocolate cakes) I found in Hungarian bakeries. One of my first jobs was at a company that made desserts for restaurants, where we prepared, among other things, "chocolate pâté" for the River Café. It really did look like a pâté, studded with pistachios and shredded white chocolate, and it was a variation on the magnificent **CHOCOLATE MAR-QUISE** I've included in this book.

When I began to travel seriously, the chocolate discoveries were even more interesting. When friends in Paris asked me, "How can you drink the incredibly rich, thick hot chocolate at Angelina's?" I didn't always tell them that not only did I love drinking it, I enjoyed it most *with* a slice of the tearoom's BITTERSWEET CHOCOLATE TART. I remember having to catch my breath the first time I walked into the venerable Maison du Chocolat. Robert Linxe, the owner and chocolatier, gave me a tour of his candy case, a taste of each of his truffles in the precise order he thought they should be tasted. I got tears in my eyes and said,

"They're perfect." His eyes were moist also as he said, "I know." There's also a "HOUSE OF VANILLA" in Paris, but every time I've walked by, it's been empty. Need I say more?

52% of all Americans say chocolate is their favorite flavor for desserts and snacks; that's 57% of women and 48% of men. Chocolate is the single most craved food in the United States. In the year 2001, chocolate consumption in this country was over three billion pounds. *Billion!*

As the chocolate softens, the comforting, unmistakable taste transports you into a delightful world of memories. —HERVÉ BIZEUL

Chocolate is a complex mixture of flavors and textures that provide comfort and nourishment, energy and satisfaction, and a magical quality that lifts the spirit. Like no other food, it offers a taste of love and a consolation for loss. I think of it as a mental-health food, or maybe I should say an emotional-health food.

Luckily for us, the quality of chocolate available is at an all-time high. Chocolate has evolved to new heights of sophistication and refinement, with wonderful ranges in flavor, aroma, and textural characteristics. I'm fond of chocolates with more chocolate flavor and less sweetness, which means chocolate with a high percentage of cocoa liquor. No, it doesn't contain alcohol—that would be chocolate liqueur. For cooking, I can't be bothered with milk chocolate, because to me it's about milk,

not about chocolate, and the flavor is just never forceful enough. I don't mind eating milk chocolate—but only when a hunk of bittersweet or semisweet is not available. For cooking, I want deep, rich, intense dark chocolate—the same silky, powerful, complex, rich, velvety chocolate with a rounded fruitiness that I would choose to eat out of hand. I love all dark rich chocolate, including French and other European chocolates, but my current favorite is an all-American product, an artisanal chocolate made in Berkeley, CALIFORNIA. It's called Scharffen Berger, and it is wonderful for eating as well as dessert making. Another thing I love about the company is that they have packaged cocoa nibs, cracked hulled cocoa beans, the basis of all chocolate and cocoa, which have the most chocolate flavor of anything on earth. And Scharffen Berger makes one of the world's finest natural cocoas. But you should also try Valrhona and MICHAEL CLUIZEL from France; CALLEBAUT from Belgium; Droste from Holland; Lindt and TOBLER from Switzerland; GREEN & BLACKS, an organic chocolate from England; Chocolates El Rey from Venezuela; Guittard and GHIRARDELLI from San Francisco; and, of course, the supermarket chocolates, Baker's, Nestlé, and Hershey. There are many wonderful chocolates out there, and your job is to find *your* favorite.

Chocolate is a magic substance, the noblest of dessert ingredients. And isn't it magnificent that the melting point of cocoa butter is just below human body temperature, so it literally melts in your mouth? I am fooled and surprised over and over again by chocolate—I always think that I will be able to keep it in my mouth longer, but it's gone before I know it. I take a bite, get distracted, come to, and it's vanished. AND IT'S NO WONDER: the tantalizing aroma of chocolate involves more than three hundred chemical compounds and the flavor can have more than five hundred components.

My goal with the recipes in this book was to incorporate as much deep, dark, rich chocolate into each one as possible. AND YOU DON'T NEED PREVIOUS EXPERI-ENCE MAKING DESSERTS OR WORKING WITH CHOCOLATE TO MAKE THEM. I am totally confident that anyone and everyone can make luscious, delectable chocolate desserts with ease by following the recipes I offer here.

A SHORT HISTORY OF
chocolate

The cacao tree has been part of human culture for at least two thousand years. As far back as records left by early Latin American civilizations can be traced, they show that chocolate was part of daily life. Cultivated by the Mayans and Aztecs long before the arrival of European explorers, the cacao tree may have originally come from the Amazon rain forest, the Orinoco Valley of Venezuela, or the Chiapa district of Mexico. The Mayans called it **cacahuaquchtl,** or "tree"—as far as they were concerned, there was no other tree worth naming. They believed that the tree belonged to the gods and that its pods were an offering from the gods to man. Cacao pods frequently appear in their texts, which show the gods performing various religious rit-uals involving the pods and often refer to cacao as the gods' food. The Mayans are believed to have been the first to consume chocolate, both as a por-ridge they made with cornmeal and as a thinner con-coction for drinking.

The ancient Aztec civilization used cacao seeds and beans as currency; according to a sixteenth-century Spanish chronicle, a rabbit was worth ten beans and a mule fifty. It's possible the Aztecs first saw monkeys and squirrels eating the refreshing white pulp around the beans and decided to try it themselves. They went on from there to an invigo-rating drink made from a paste of the roasted beans. Columbus was probably the first European to encounter chocolate, but when he took the beans back to King Ferdinand and Queen Isabella, they underestimated the importance of the "brown gold."

The explorer Cortés reportedly found the Aztec Indians using the beans to prepare the royal drink of the realm and was served some in 1519 by the Emperor Montezuma, who was said to drink fifty or more portions daily. Because it was very bitter to their taste, when the first large supplies of cocoa beans were brought back to Spain in 1528,

From the court of Montezuma to the court of Spain— so began the odyssey of chocolate, for of all the foods discovered in the New World, it was chocolate that underwent the most dramatic transformation. It left its home a bitter stimulant drink and returned as a sweet confection, a food of pleasure, a food of fun. —ELISABETH ROZIN, *Blue Corn and Chocolate*

the Spanish began to sweeten the beverage they made with cane sugar and to serve it hot. They also sometimes added other flavorings, such as cinnamon, black pepper, anise, nutmeg, cloves, lemon peel, orange-flower water, and even powdered dried rose petals. Cocoa became a popular drink of the Spanish aristocracy, and Spain began to plant cacao trees in its colonies, giving them a very profitable business selling to other countries on the Continent. For roughly a century, cocoa remained a Spanish drink, and a Spanish secret. Eventually the secret of how to process the cocoa beans was revealed, and it was not long before chocolate was acclaimed throughout Europe as a delicious, health-giving food. Because chocolate was expensive, however, hot chocolate remained at first a drink of royalty and aristocrats. It was drunk in the fashionable court of France, and the

vogue for hot chocolate continued at Versailles under Louis XIV and then under Louis XV.

The taste for chocolate then spread across the Channel to Great Britain, and in 1657 the first of many famous English chocolate houses opened. Italian doctors used the drink as a restorative, and the first chocolate factories were established by apothecaries in the 1700s, to make medicinal chocolates.

By 1730, chocolate had dropped in price to within financial reach of most. And the machinery that was developed in the early nineteenth century, as part of the Industrial Revolution, opened the way for production of chocolate in larger quantities at lower cost. The invention of the cocoa press reduced prices even further and helped to improve the quality of the beverage. From then on, drinking chocolate had more of the smooth consistency and pleasing flavor it has today. The price of sugar also fell dramatically, and that, combined with a general rise in living standards across Europe, assured the democratization of chocolate. By the early twentieth century, chocolate had become an integral part of daily life in Europe.

With the ever-growing popularity of chocolate in Europe, the cultivation of cacao spread across the globe. Cacao plantations were established in many of the same areas that nations such as Britain, France, and Portugal had colonized for the spice trade.

In the American colonies, the production of chocolate quickly took hold. It was in New England, in 1764, that the first chocolate factory, called Baker's Chocolate then and now, was established in the Massachusetts Bay Colony, in what is now the city of Dorchester.

FROM cacao TO chocolate

Chocolate bars do not grow on cacao trees, but cacao pods do. During and after harvesting, they undergo a series of complex transformations to yield the chocolate we enjoy using to prepare desserts and eating out of hand.

The distinctive flavor profiles of different chocolates can vary greatly depending on the microclimate where the beans were grown, how skillfully they were nurtured and harvested, and their treatment during the critical fermentation and drying process. Chocolate making is an art as well as a science, and chocolate makers keep secret the roasting temperatures used, the time given to "conching" (the action that results in fine-flavored, smooth, and mellow chocolate; see page 15 for more detail), and the exact proportions in their formulations, which is why no two manufacturers' chocolates taste the same. But all manufacturers follow the same general procedures.

the cacao tree

All chocolate begins with the cacao tree. Sensitive and delicate, the trees thrive only in moist tropical climates near the equator, in a belt around the earth's middle. Cacao trees will not grow at too high an altitude, nor in a place that is too cold or too dry, and they need to be shaded from the strong tropical sun and sheltered from the wind. (They also need protection from the wild animals that delight in picking the pods.) The trees like considerable but well-distributed rainfall and heavy but well-drained soil, and their ideal growing temperature is 80 degrees Fahrenheit.

The Latin name of the cacao tree, a perennial evergreen of the cola family, is *theobroma*, or, literally, "food of the gods." The tree grows straight and slender, with few branches, to a height of between fifteen and sixty feet in the wild; in cultivation, the height is kept to between thirteen and thirty-three feet. THE TREE FLOWERS AND FRUITS CONSTANTLY AND SIMULTANEOUSLY, AND IT DIFFERS FROM ALL OTHERS IN THAT ITS flowers and fruit (the cacao pods) cluster on both the trunk and its larger branches, GROWING STRAIGHT OUT OF RAISED CUSHIONS NO LONGER THAN AN INCH RATHER THAN ON STEMS LIKE APPLES AND OTHER FAMILIAR FRUITS. The flowers must be pollinated before the tree can produce the pods; tiny flies are the main natural pollinators, but the trees can also be pollinated by hand. After pollination, the flowers take about five months to develop into pods.

> Cacao is the third largest agricultural export crop in the world, following coffee and sugar.

By assessing the color of a pod and the sound it makes when tapped, a skilled picker can tell if it is ripe or not. The ripened pods, oval and eight to fourteen inches long, range in color from yellow or green to red, maroon, or violet. Looking something like small footballs, they are deeply ridged and often speckled with multicolored flecks. One British writer described a cacao walk, or grove, viewed from above as like... "looking at a miniature forest hung with thousands of golden lamps."

There is nothing I like better than tropical fruits. I've even planned vacations around the fruits available in a specific region. I adore many exotic fruits of the tropics—durians, mangosteens, and salak, among others—but my favorite is **chocolate. I've been lucky enough to see fresh cacao pods,** and the first time I did, I was thrilled and very surprised at how beautiful they were; **they were a stunning glowing golden yellow,** and the fragrance made me think of "fresh chocolate." I wanted to take one home with me. Split open, the pod had the same aroma as a chocolate bar, but with a delicate, flowery, and refreshing element that was irresistible: **chocolate as a fruit, without the richness of chocolate as we know it.** I did steal a taste of the white pulp around the cacao beans, and it tasted just like it smelled. I was captivated, and if you ever have the opportunity to see, feel, smell, and taste fresh chocolate, seize it!

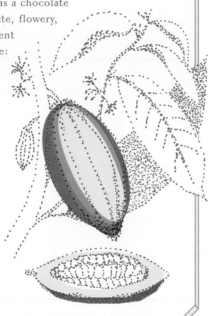

and the annual yield of a cacao tree is between seven and eight pounds of dried beans, enough for one to two and a half pounds of finished chocolate. A tree can produce fruit for seventy-five to one hundred years or more—some trees are known to be over two hundred years old—but after twenty-five years, the economic usefulness of a tree is generally considered at an end.

Since cacao trees cross-pollinate freely, there is a wide range of varieties and subvarieties, but they can be reduced to three main classifications, each with a distinctive flavor profile. The soft, thin-skinned pods of the **Criollo** from Venezuela or Java have a light color and a unique, pleasing aroma. The more plentiful rich **Forastero** of Brazil, Ghana, and the Ivory Coast, which is easier to cultivate, has a thick-walled pod and a pungent aroma. The fine-flavored, aromatic **Trinitario** is believed to be a natural cross between strains of the other two. In the Western Hemisphere, plantations of just one species are uncommon; even single trees with the characteristics only of a specific type are rare. Ninety percent of the international crop is Forastero; the prized Criollo and the Trinitario are not only more expensive, but also more distinctive, with full, aromatic flavors. The higher percentage of these two beans in any chocolate, the more interesting and elegant its flavor will be, and their addition can mean the difference between a rich, complex chocolate and a blunt, one-dimensional one.

Each pod contains twenty-five to seventy-five seeds, or beans, arranged in five densely packed rows around a central placenta and enveloped in a whitish pulp that is both sweet and slightly acid, similar in flavor and texture to lychee fruit but with that amazing chocolate aroma. The dried beans from an average pod weigh less than two ounces,

THE CRIOLLO (*Creole* in Spanish, which means "native") is the original cacao tree of the Mayan civilization in Mexico, delicate and hence relatively rare. Its yields are low and it is more susceptible to disease than the Forastero bean. Known as "the prince of cacaos," it is valued for its fruity flavor and fine acidity. Highly perfumed, subtle and aromatic in flavor, it varies greatly depending on the region of production; it is grown in Venezuela, Madagascar, and Indonesia. Criollo beans are seldom used alone, but even in small quantities will enhance the quality of a blend.

THE FORASTERO ("foreigner" in Spanish) originated in the high Amazon but is now grown in Africa, where it is the predominant variety, and throughout the world. Hardier, higher-yielding, and easier to cultivate than the Criollo, it is used in just about every blend of chocolate made. The African varieties are thought to be fairly ordinary, but there are some finer, more distinguished varieties found in Brazil, Ecuador, Trinidad, and Venezuela.

THE TRINITARIO takes its elegant aroma from the Criollo and its robust constitution from the Forastero. The name actually refers to many hybrids, not just a single variety. First cultivated in Trinidad, Trinitario trees are now also grown in Latin America, Sri Lanka, and Indonesia.

harvest

At harvesttime, because the tall trees are too fragile for pickers to climb, skilled workers armed with long-handled steel knives snip the pods from even the topmost branches without piercing the delicate bark. Machetes are used to remove pods from the lower trunk and branches. With one or two whacks of their machetes, the workers break them open, then scoop out the cocoa beans and discard the husks and inner membrane. Soon after the pods are opened, the beans change color, from ivory to a deep lavender or purple.

fermentation

Fermentation is the first crucial stage in developing beans of superior quality. The cacao beans, with the fleshy pulp still clinging to them, are placed in boxes or baskets to ferment for from two to nine days, depending on the humidity. Bacteria and yeasts present in the air multiply on the sugary pulp, causing it to decompose into acetic acid (the main component of vinegar) and turn to alcohol, much as the sugar in wine grapes does. Their color changes from purple to brown and the familiar chocolate aroma begins to emerge. As the flavor develops, the bitterness subsides, and the seeds turn a rich shade of russet, a sign to the farmer that they are ready to be dried.

drying

Drying concentrates the flavors by evaporating the water content. The beans may be dried on trays or bamboo matting in the sun, over a low fire, or by hot air pipes indoors. The beans are turned often so they can dry thoroughly and evenly. Drying takes from ten to twenty days, and then the beans are classified by size for pricing purposes, poured into huge sacks stamped with the grower's name, and transported to chocolate factories all over the world.

roasting

Roasting develops the flavor and aroma of the beans, enriches their color, and dries the husks surrounding the **nibs,** the edible part of the bean, making their removal easier. Roasting dries the nibs as well so they will be ready for grinding and refining. The degree of roasting is critical: overdoing it destroys the natural flavor of the bean and produces a bitter result, while underroasting fails to eradicate the inherent bitterness of the raw bean. The temperature and duration of the roasting must be finely calculated to suit the particular beans; mild varieties are usually roasted at a lower temperature than stronger ones. Beans destined for cocoa powder may be roasted longer than those for chocolate. Roasting may take from half an hour to two hours; European makers generally roast for longer periods of time at lower temperatures to develop better flavor.

husking

The husking and winnowing process cracks open the beans and blows the lighter husks away from the heavier pieces. Then the beans are cracked into small irregular pieces, the nibs. The nibs are ground, the fat they contain—cocoa butter—is liquefied, and the ground nibs and the butter are transformed into the rich brown mass called chocolate liquor. Despite its name, the paste does not contain alcohol, and it is solid at room temperature.

cocoa

At this point, the chocolate liquor can be used for either cocoa powder or chocolate. Cocoa is made by removing the cocoa butter from the chocolate liquor under hydraulic pressure. After the cocoa butter is removed, the resulting substance is cooled, pulverized, and sifted until it is recognizable as unsweetened cocoa powder.

chocolate

To make chocolate, chocolate liquor from different varieties or harvests of beans is selected, depending on the desired final flavor, and blended together. Other ingredients, such as sugar, lecithin, and vanilla may be added at this point.

The blended mixture is then ground and kneaded by machine in a process called **conching**. Developed in Switzerland by Rodolphe Lindt, conching is essential for reducing the bitterness and acidity of the blended paste. It breaks up any cocoa butter solids and gives the chocolate its balance, character, and final texture. By aerating the chocolate and ridding it of residual moisture and volatile acids, conching gives it a satiny texture and a smooth harmonious flavor. The length of time chocolate is conched depends on the quality a manufacturer is seeking—the longer the conching, the better the chocolate (but some industrial manufacturers skip it altogether). Conching may last anywhere from twelve to seventy-two hours. The first stage is dry conching: friction is used to smooth the cocoa and sugar particles. Next is wet conching, when cocoa butter and sometimes lecithin are added to smooth it further. Once tempered, cooled, and hardened, the conched chocolate liquor will be chocolate.

tempering

The still-liquid conched chocolate is tempered for sheen, smooth texture, and keeping qualities. The tempering process involves raising and then lowering the temperature of the chocolate to stabilize the cocoa butter crystals. It gives chocolate its characteristic snap, gloss, and smooth texture and prevents bloom (see page 22); it also makes it easier to unmold the formed chocolate. The tempered chocolate may be poured into molds of many shapes and sizes. Once cooled and hardened, the bars are removed from their molds, wrapped, and packed for shipment.

THE **forms** OF **chocolate**

The u.s. FOOD AND DRUG ADMINISTRATION'S standards of identity for chocolate are based on the percentages of key ingredients—mainly chocolate liquor and sugar—it contains. Each company that manufactures chocolate has its own formula, but all must comply with the standards of identity for each product.

unsweetened chocolate

Unsweetened chocolate is pure unadulterated chocolate liquor, the ground cocoa bean nibs and nothing else. Sometimes labeled "99% chocolate," it has a very intense chocolate flavor, but don't even think of eating it out of hand, no matter how much you love chocolate—it is painfully harsh and bitter. I use it very infrequently, mostly for brownies, because I see no reason to keep chocolate around the house if you can't eat it as is!

sweetened dark chocolate

The category of sweetened dark chocolate includes both bittersweet and semisweet chocolate. Within its extremely broad guidelines, these chocolates can vary greatly in terms of amounts of sugar, added cocoa butter, lecithin, flavorings such as vanilla, and total amount of chocolate liquor. There is no official distinction between bittersweet and semisweet chocolate, though generally bittersweet is less sweet than semisweet because it contains more chocolate liquor. However, one manufacturer's bittersweet may be another's semisweet. The more bitter the chocolate, the more intense the chocolate flavor, and the more you can taste its fruitiness, because there is less sugar to mask it. Interchangeable in most recipes, bittersweet and semisweet chocolate are used for baking and candy making and are excellent eating chocolates as well.

Today you'll see more chocolates that note the percentage (by weight) of chocolate liquor they contain. These percentages range from about 55 to 60 percent for semisweet and from 60 to 80 percent for bittersweet. A chocolate labeled "70%," for example, means that it contains about 30 percent sugar, with about 1 percent vanilla and

Why Are Some Chocolates So Much More Expensive than Others? Quality chocolate makers select high-quality cocoa beans and use only beans that have undergone a thorough fermentation. The different qualities they look for in the beans they purchase result from extra time and effort on the part of the growers, adding in turn to their cost. These producers also make chocolate in batches far smaller than most industrially manufactured chocolates, and they pay close personal attention to detail. They usually use many different beans to blend their bittersweet chocolate; they might, for example, include some beans from Mexico for their citric smell, others from Ghana for their length and depth of flavor, still others from Papua New Guinea for their sharp acidity and tannins, and so forth. These makers even use high-quality whole vanilla beans from Madagascar and Tahiti rather than extract or artificial vanillin. Industrially produced chocolates have none of the complexities and nuances of these "artisanal" chocolates.

Lecithin, a fat obtained from soybeans, is used as a natural stabilizer and emulsifier in the manufacture of chocolate; it does not affect the taste. **Cocoa butter,** the fat extracted from cocoa beans when chocolate and cocoa powder are made, contributes to the flavor, texture, sheen, and meltability of chocolate. When you're buying dark sweetened chocolate, look for one that contains cocoa butter and no other fat except lecithin as a stabilizer.

soy lecithin. (Always buy chocolate made with real vanilla, not artificial vanillin.)

Be aware that the higher the percentage of chocolate liquor, the less stable the chocolate is. If you use one of the very high percentage, or "extreme," chocolates to make a ganache, for example, it may separate. And FLOURLESS CHOCOLATE CAKE made with a "70%" chocolate will taste profoundly more intense than one made with a 40 or 50% chocolate. If you're substituting a high-percentage chocolate for a more standard one in a baking recipe, you might add a little extra sugar. Lower-percentage chocolates are sometimes described as "calmer," because they don't separate as easily.

cocoa powder

There are two basic types of cocoa powder, natural and Dutch-process. **NATURAL,** or nonalkalized, is the type Americans are most familiar with (Hershey's is the most popular brand, although the company is now making an alkalized version as well). Natural cocoa is naturally acidic with the fruitiness of cocoa beans, light brown in color, and pleasantly bitter, with a deep chocolate flavor. **DUTCH-PROCESS** cocoa is traditionally thought of as European-style. During processing, the powder is treated with an alkali (usually potassium carbonate) to reduce its natural acidity, making the cocoa less bitter and mellowing the flavor. Dutch-process cocoa (so-called in honor of its inventor, Coenraad van Houten, a Dutchman) is darker than natural cocoa.

Many people mistakenly assume that alkalized cocoa powder is better than natural cocoa powder. It is not better, just different. Dutch-processing first came into use in part because of manufacturers who were using poorly fermented, lower-quality cocoa beans for making cocoa powder; they could simply chemically treat any flavor problems with alkali to cover them up. But well-fermented high-quality beans are naturally mild, and untreated natural cocoa powder allows their inherent fruitiness and full flavor to emerge; thus natural cocoa can be of very high quality. And, contrary to what your eyes might tell you, dark cocoas often have less chocolate flavor than lighter ones. Another common misconception is that alkalized cocoa powder dissolves more easily in a liquid than nonalkalized; in fact, it is the fineness of the particles that determines how well the cocoa powder can be dissolved.

In recipes that use baking soda, you want to use natural cocoa powder; the combination of the acid in the cocoa with the soda will create a leavening action that makes a batter rise during baking. In recipes that call for baking powder as the primary leavener, use Dutch-process cocoa. (If alkalized cocoa is combined with baking soda, another alkali, it will create an overabundance of alkali in the batter and, as a result, the batter will not rise properly and the cake will have a soapy taste.) In recipes with no leavening, you can use either one.

milk chocolate

Milk chocolate, obviously, contains milk, occasionally in the form of a condensed liquid, but usually as a concentrated dry powder that replaces some of the cocoa solids, giving the chocolate a smooth taste and texture. It has significantly less chocolate liquor than bittersweet or semisweet chocolate and more sugar; and, by law, it must contain at least 12 percent milk solids, which is why it is considerably lighter in color and less intensely chocolate than dark chocolates. Milk chocolate cannot be substituted for a bittersweet or semisweet chocolate in recipes. It is difficult to use in cooking because it is very sensitive to heat, and it is most suitable for eating out of hand.

white chocolate

Simply put, it doesn't exist: it may be white, but it's not chocolate. The FDA does not consider it chocolate, because it contains no chocolate liquor, only cocoa butter. (Don't confuse it with white confectionery coating, which contains vegetable fat rather than cocoa butter.) It also contains sugar, dairy products, an emulsifier, and vanilla. It is the sweetest type of chocolate and the most difficult to work with because the high proportion of cocoa butter and dairy products make it temperamental and extremely sensitive to heat.

> White chocolate has great appeal for those who find that color and flavor interfere with the experience of texture.
> —SANDRA BOYNTON, *Chocolate the Consuming Passion*

chocolate chips

Use chocolate chips only when they are called for in a recipe. Formulated to retain their shape when baked, they do not melt easily, and they are not right for other tasks. They also contain less cocoa butter than other chocolates. They should not be substituted for semisweet or bittersweet chocolate.

nibs

Nibs are cracked roasted husked cocoa beans. They are unsweetened, pleasantly bitter, and as intensely chocolate as any substance. Their flavor is marvelously deep and powerful, dry and astringent. They are nut-like or coffee bean–like, and they have fruit flavors, acidity, tannins, and spicy flavors like cinnamon and clove. Because they have no sugar, their flavors are easier to discern on the tongue than chocolate.

If nibs are new to you, they may take some getting used to, but I loved them on first taste. To appreciate them, you might have to forget that you're dealing with chocolate, because so much of how we perceive chocolate is through memory and imagination, and much of that can be about texture. But most true chocolate lovers adore nibs. You can use nibs as you would nuts; they are similar in that both are high in fat and have lots of flavor. Generally, you should use about half the amount of nibs as you would nuts, but you can figure out your own proportion. They are crunchier than nuts and won't get soggy in liquid. You might also use them as you would chocolate chips, or in combination with chips. Infusing them in a liquid, such as heavy cream, is a great way to get flavor from nibs. Or grind them to a powder, or coarsely grind them, or anything in between, and use them as an ingredient or a garnish. Scharffen Berger was the first to market nibs to consumers, and their very high quality nibs are packed in 6-ounce tins, which contain a generous 1½ cups. They are available in many supermarkets and in specialty foods stores.

Store nibs well wrapped in a cool, dry place. If you'd like to store them for a longer time, freeze them in an airtight container.

HOW TO MAKE CHOCOLATE USING NIBS

This is my favorite culinary science experiment.

GRIND nibs with granulated sugar to a fine paste in a clean coffee grinder. For bittersweet chocolate, use about ⅔ **cup cocoa nibs** and ⅓ **cup sugar.** When the paste is as fine as you can make it, warm it in a heatproof bowl set over a saucepan of about 1½ inches of nearly simmering water to melt the cocoa butter the nibs contain. You've made chocolate! You can then mold the chocolate or pour it into a small dish to cool and harden.

SOME IDEAS FOR USING NIBS

Top ice cream, sorbet, sundaes, or coupes with a coarse or fine dusting of nibs. Or sprinkle on frosted cakes or creamy puddings.

Sprinkle coarsely ground nibs over strawberries, raspberries, and/or blackberries sweetened with a little sugar or over fresh or poached pears or peaches.

Add nibs to a peanut butter and honey sandwich.

Stir into pancake or waffle batter. Or cake batter. Or quick bread batter.

Use nibs in savory salads as you would nuts.

Add nibs to chocolate mousse or other smooth, creamy treats.

Add to cookie doughs, such as chocolate chip and almost any biscotti.

Add just a few to your coffee beans when grinding them.

Sprinkle finely ground nibs over a cappuccino.

Steep nibs in the liquid, such as heavy cream or milk, that you will be using to make custards, puddings, or sauces or that you will chill and whip for serving. Strain before using.

For a different kind of chocolate chip, add nibs to ice cream toward the end of the freezing process.

chocolate AND health

Dark chocolate may be the next health food (milk chocolate and white chocolate don't have the same properties). It is loaded with antioxidants—it has even more than strawberries. And, like red wine or tea, chocolate can raise good cholesterol, reduce bad cholesterol, and prevent plaque formation in your circulatory system.

It has been shown as proof positive that carefully prepared chocolate is as healthful a food as it is pleasant; that it is nourishing and easily digested; that it does not cause the same harmful effects to feminine beauty that are blamed on coffee, but is on the contrary a remedy for them. —JEAN-ANTHELME BRILLAT-SAVARIN

Definitely a MOOD ENHANCER, chocolate contains phenylethylamine, WHICH IS SAID TO MIMIC THE FEELING PEOPLE HAVE WHEN THEY ARE IN LOVE. Chocolate will unfailingly produce a sensation of mild euphoria and well-being, alleviate depression, and refresh the spirits. The very tasting of it encourages the secretion of endorphins, a form of morphine produced by the body. When released into the blood stream, endorphins lift the mood, creating positive energy and feelings. Chocolate also boosts the production of calming serotonin.

Chocolate contains MAGNESIUM, to ease stress and muscular contractions, and CAFFEINE and THEO-BROMINE, to stimulate the mind and body and combat fatigue. It has a good amount of IRON and POTAS-SIUM, as well as traces of several vitamins. That iron,

chocolate is the "Prozac of plants."
—DEBORAH WATERHOUSE, *Why Women Need Chocolate*

which helps transport oxygen to the brain, may result in greater mental alertness. The theobromine stimulates the kidneys as a mild diuretic. Chocolate also acts as a stimulant on the central nervous system, with an effect similar to that of coffee.

In short, chocolate may not be the forbidden pleasure some of us tend to think it is. Since the fourth century, it has been used for its therapeutic values, both as a stimulant and as a source of comfort and pleasure.

In the seventeenth and eighteenth centuries, great claims for its health-giving properties were made by manufacturers, who touted it as an antidote to exhaustion and weakness, and soldiers, scholars, and clerics all used it to keep themselves going. The fat in chocolate does, in fact, provide fuel for the body, and that fat means that chocolate is digested slowly, maintaining the feeling of satisfaction.

CHOCOLATE MYTHS   Research shows that, contrary to popular opinion, chocolate does not cause migraines, (eating it may in fact help with the pain of one). Nor does chocolate cause indigestion or liver disorders. There is no correlation between acne and chocolate. And allergic reactions to chocolate are extremely rare.

HOW TO **taste chocolate**

I learned much of this from Carole Bloom and from Maricel Presilla. Thank you!

Enjoy a fun but serious tasting of chocolate with friends. Try tasting six or so brands of the same type of chocolate, bittersweet, for example. (Unlike a wine tasting you'll never have to spit!) Tasting different chocolates next to each other can be much more interesting and revealing than tasting just one.

ALWAYS TASTE PLAIN CHOCOLATE, without nuts or other such ingredients. Have the chocolate at room temperature; cold will mask its flavor.

LOOK AT THE CHOCOLATE: It should be evenly colored with a slight sheen and an even, glossy surface. It should be smooth, uniform, clean, and flawless. Dark chocolate should be very dark, possibly with faint red highlights.

HOLD A PIECE OF CHOCOLATE BETWEEN YOUR THUMB AND FOREFINGER FOR A FEW SECONDS, then look to see if you've made fingerprints on it. If you have, it's a good sign: it indicates that the chocolate contains cocoa butter instead of vegetable oil (inferior chocolates made with vegetable oil will leave a greasy feeling in your mouth). The cocoa butter in good chocolate melts at just below body temperature, so the chocolate should just barely begin to melt when handled.

INHALE THE FRAGRANCE OF THE CHOCOLATE, as you would that of a glass of wine. Chocolate should have a strong aroma—a complex aroma is best—and there should be no off odors. The fragrance should be sweet but not too sweet, with a slightly fruity and/or floral element; citrus, berries, vanilla, cherries, and even caramel are good notes. Note whether the aroma is faint or intense, and if it comes on all at once or builds over time. It should entice you to taste the chocolate.

BREAK OFF A CHUNK OF THE CHOCOLATE. It should break firmly and cleanly with a faint snap and be velvety smooth in texture, not grainy. Chew the chocolate just to break it up. It should begin to melt and to melt evenly. It should have resistance to your teeth and should not crumble, splinter, bend, or stretch.

PRESS A PIECE OR PIECES OF THE CHOCOLATE TO THE ROOF OF YOUR MOUTH WITH YOUR TONGUE, and wait about twenty-five seconds to allow it to melt over your tongue. The chocolate should be very smooth and creamy, and it should quickly turn to a silky liquid.

AS THE CHOCOLATE PASSES OVER YOUR TASTE BUDS, ASK YOURSELF THESE QUESTIONS: Is there a fruit flavor there, such as berry or citrus, cherries, or even dried apricot? Or is there a caramel, vanilla, or nutty flavor? All of those are good. Does the flavor stay with you, lasting for as long as a minute? If there is a vanilla flavor, does it round out the complex flavors of the chocolate or does it taste strong? Does the chocolate have a pleasant, clean finish? Does it have a long or short finish; if it has a long finish, does it have highs and lows? Is the flavor simple and direct?

THEN CONTINUE WITH THE OTHER CHOCOLATES, AND ENJOY THEM ALL!

chocolate basics

storage

Chocolate's biggest enemies are moisture, strong odors, heat, and light, and it does not respond well to fluctuations in temperature or humidity. Its ideal storage environment is 65 degrees Fahrenheit and 50 percent humidity, away from strong smells and with good air circulation. I buy my chocolate in five-kilo blocks, break it up, and store it in self-sealing plastic bags at room temperature, unless the weather is very hot and humid. When it is, I find the coolest place I've got outside of the refrigerator, usually my pantry, which is well insulated and stays fairly cool. I prefer plastic bags to aluminum foil because they can be tightly sealed and the chocolate is better protected.

If chocolate is stored at warmer temperatures, it may get what is called "fat bloom," which occurs when the cocoa butter rises to the surface, resulting in grayish marks. "Sugar bloom" may result when chocolate is stored under damp conditions, and it leaves the chocolate feeling rough. Neither type of bloom will affect the quality of the chocolate if it is to be melted and used in baking or cooking.

If chocolate is stored in the refrigerator or the freezer, it will sweat when brought to room temperature and will shatter rather than snap when broken. If you must refrigerate or freeze chocolate, to avoid problems with condensation when melting the chocolate, always allow it to come to room temperature, still wrapped, before breaking or chopping it.

For long-term storage, chocolate keeps better as a slab than in little pieces. Dark chocolate has a shelf life of at least a year.

chopping chocolate

Always use a dry cutting board and a sharp heavy knife when chopping chocolate. It's easiest if you begin chopping from a corner of the chocolate.

melting chocolate

For the smoothest results, melt chocolate slowly and gently. Chocolate melts at a lower temperature than many other solids, and it needs only to get warm to melt. Tend it closely while it's melting, as it can scorch in a split second—and that's not pretty, or pleasant.

There are several ways to melt chocolate: the three best ways are the oven, the microwave, or the top of a double boiler or heatproof bowl set over a saucepan of nearly simmering water. Direct heat is not recommended unless the chocolate is being melted with another ingredient like cream or butter, as it can scorch so easily.

Ninety-nine percent of the time I melt my chocolate in a stainless-steel bowl set over a saucepan of about an inch and a half of nearly simmering water. The water level is important because you don't want the hot water to touch the bottom of the bowl. I find this the fastest and safest way to melt any amount of chocolate, and I like that I can see it at all times. By keeping the heat very low, I can relax enough about the chocolate melting to do other preparation for the dessert while I am waiting. If there is a lot to do for a recipe, I sometimes bring the water to a simmer and turn off the heat; when I come back to it later, the chocolate will have melted. With the heat off or very low, I don't need to worry about the chocolate getting too hot or steam from the water getting into it (see "Chocolate and Liquid" below).

Always break or chop the chocolate into small-ish pieces (try for half an inch) so that it melts more quickly and evenly. And stir well and often.

Many dessert professionals melt chocolate in a low oven, in a shallow baking pan or dish. The melting time will depend on the amount of chocolate and the size of the pieces, but be sure to stir it occasionally until it is completely melted and smooth. It's not my favorite method, because my oven, unlike those in professional kitchens, isn't always already on, and I can't see the chocolate as it melts.

Melting chocolate in the microwave is appropriate only for small amounts, no more than a few ounces at a time. If you're melting in a microwave, it is especially important to cut the chocolate into small, even-sized pieces. Use medium or low power, never high. Timing will depend on the oven and type and amount of chocolate being melted. Keep in mind that chocolate melted in the microwave won't look melted until it's stirred, so make sure to check and stir it frequently.

However you choose to melt your chocolate, never cover it while it is melting. Condensation forming under the lid could drop into the chocolate and cause it to seize (see below). Likewise, wipe the walls of the microwave dry if necessary before melting chocolate, because it can act as a big steamer.

chocolate and liquid

It is a peculiar quality of chocolate that it can be melted with liquid, but if even a drop of liquid is added to already melted chocolate, it may cause it to "seize," meaning it will clump, harden, and become dry and grainy. The same thing will happen if cold liquid is added to warm chocolate or if chocolate is melted with too little liquid. If this happens, throw out the seized chocolate and begin again. Recommended remedies, such as adding vegetable shortening, rarely correct the problem.

When you're melting chocolate in a bowl over a saucepan, make certain the bowl fits tightly so steam won't leak out and settle on the surface of the chocolate.

Always cool melted chocolate before adding it to a batter or dough; adding it hot could affect the texture of the final product. Having all ingredients at a similar temperature helps guard against blending problems.

CHOCOLATE WEIGHTS TO VOLUME

8 ounces solid chocolate, melted = ¾ cup

1 pound solid chocolate, melted = 1½ cups

baking basics

You need not be a dedicated or experienced cook or baker to produce delicious results. If your first efforts are not perfect to look at, you will find the encouragement to try again when everyone who tastes them mentions how delicious they are. Most important, it's vital that you have fun, enjoy what you are doing, and not be anxious about the results.

ALL THE RECIPES IN THIS BOOK ARE TRIED AND TESTED, and changing the ingredients or method will give different results. I suggest you follow the recipes carefully to begin with, and you will soon discover for yourself those than can easily be varied and how you might want to vary them.

READ THE ENTIRE RECIPE BEFORE YOU BEGIN. Then assemble the ingredients and equipment. Check to see if any ingredients need to be brought to room temperature.

ALWAYS USE HIGH-QUALITY INGREDIENTS, including the best chocolate you can afford.

USE THE APPROPRIATE MEASURING CUPS FOR DRY AND LIQUID INGREDIENTS, and measure carefully. For liquids, use glass measuring cups with spouts. For dry ingredients, use metal cups that can be leveled off with a knife or spatula.

BAKED GOODS SHOULD BE BAKED IN THE MIDDLE OF THE OVEN unless otherwise indicated.

MOST CAKES, PIES, AND TARTS SHOULD BE COOLED ON WIRE RACKS (in or out of the pan, depending on the recipe), as should cookies, to prevent the bottoms from becoming soggy.

ingredients

BUTTER Opt for the fullness of flavor and creaminess of butter when making chocolate desserts. Margarine doesn't taste good, it has an unpleasant mouth-feel, and it is loaded with trans-fats (the most unhealthy fats of all). Using butter is especially important in brownies, cookies, and other baked chocolate desserts, where it contributes flavor, moistness, and crumb texture. Use unsalted or "sweet" butter; salted butter is too salty for chocolate desserts. For storage of longer than a week or so, freeze it. (If you are observing Jewish dietary laws, substitute pareve margarine for butter for nondairy meals. If you must use margarine instead of butter, use it in its least processed states; that is, don't use tub margarine, spreads, or butter substitutes, which contain more water than stick margarine and are not made for baking.)

BAKING POWDER AND BAKING SODA Baking soda, pure bicarbonate of soda, is activated when mixed with liquid that is acidic, such as buttermilk. Baking powder, a combination of bicarbonate of soda, cream of tartar, and cornstarch, works no matter what liquid it's mixed with, as the cream of tartar provides the acidity. Don't let a batter made with baking powder and/or baking soda sit around before baking it, or you won't get optimal service from the leavener. Check the expiration dates on the package before using, and be precise in your measuring, as too little or too much will not give the desired result.

EGGS Use fresh Grade AA large eggs for these recipes; using a different size may mean disappointing results. Always purchase eggs from a refrigerated case and keep them refrigerated at home.

NUTS Nuts, including almonds, Brazil nuts, hazelnuts, cashews, macadamias, peanuts, pistachios, pecans, and walnuts, all marry delightfully with chocolate, whether they are whole, chopped, slivered, ground, or sliced. Unfortunately, nuts go rancid quickly. For the longest life, buy whole raw nuts, and for long-term storage, store nuts in a self-sealing plastic bag in the freezer, where they will keep for up to six months. Toast nuts just before using them, to bring out more flavor and a wonderful crunch. Always taste nuts before adding them to a recipe; the flavor of a rancid or moldy nut will ruin a dessert.

INSTANT ESPRESSO POWDER The one I use is made by Medaglia D'Oro; it is available in most supermarkets.

VANILLA AND **OTHER EXTRACTS** There is no quicker way to ruin a dessert than by using harsh artificially flavored extracts. Vanilla and other extracts must be the real thing. Allow hot mixtures and other ingredients to cool before adding vanilla or another extract. These have an alcohol base, and heat will release not only the fragrance, but the flavor as well.

equipment

ELECTRIC MIXERS I used a hand-held mixer for every recipe in this book that calls for a mixer. If you have a heavy-duty standing mixer, feel free to use it, but you don't need one for any of the recipes.

RUBBER SPATULAS One of the greatest recent advances in kitchen equipment is the development of heat-resistant rubber spatulas. Not having to worry about a meltdown is quite wonderful. Now you can also use them for cooking, as well as for scraping down bowls while mixing, folding ingredients together, and dozens of other tasks.

MIXING BOWLS It's impossible to have too many mixing bowls. Stainless-steel bowls are great for using as an improvised double boiler over a pan of hot water. Glass bowls are essential for use in the microwave, for melting chocolate or butter. For dessert making, you'll need at least one very large bowl for beating egg whites, cream, and the like. I find deep bowls far more versatile than shallower ones.

ROLLING PIN The type you use is really a matter of personal taste. Your grandmother's traditional pin, a wooden dowel type, or a heavy ball-bearing pin with handles: any of these will be great.

STRAINERS I use these often, to strain out tiny bits of overcooked egg or whatever else might get in the way of the perfect smoothness of a finished dessert. Have a few on hand, large and small, coarse and fine. A small fine strainer is perfect for sifting confectioners' sugar or unsweetened cocoa powder over a dessert just before serving.

SIFTER I don't use a sifter for sifting. I use a coarse strainer. Use whichever you like, but for the best crumb and for accurate measuring, don't skip the sifting step when a recipe specifies it.

WHISKS These are very handy kitchen tools. Find one that feels well balanced and comfortable in your hand. I often use a whisk to aerate and mix the dry ingredients; it's quicker and easier than sifting when sifting is really not necessary. I also use whisks for folding one component of a dish into another. Have both large and small whisks on hand.

BAKING PANS Use shiny, not dark, baking pans. Baking sheets should fit into your oven with at least two inches of space between them and the oven walls so the heat can circulate freely.

WIRE RACKS A couple of large, sturdy wire racks are essential for cooling baked goods.

ICE CREAM MACHINES There are now many reasonably priced machines available (at only about fifty dollars) that don't require the messy use of salt and ice, making the preparation of frozen desserts easy enough for a school night. Look for one that makes at least 1 quart.

tips, techniques, and tricks of the trade

BEATING EGG WHITES Always use impeccably clean bowls and beaters. If I'm not absolutely confident that no vestige of egg yolk or other fat is lurking, I give the beaters and bowl a quick wash with a splash of vinegar and water. I've found it's best to beat at medium speed until the whites are foamy, then increase the speed to medium-high and beat to soft or stiff peaks, as the recipe requires. For soft peaks, beat the whites just to the point that when the beaters are lifted the whites make peaks that fall over immediately. For stiff peaks, beat until the peaks stand straight up and stay there.

CREAMING BUTTER AND SUGAR Use an electric mixer for creaming butter and sugar, and beat until the sugar is barely grainy. This can take a few minutes, so make sure to beat long enough. And make sure the butter is at room temperature when you begin.

FOLDING Folding is used to combine certain ingredients, such as whipped egg whites, with another ingredient or mixture without deflating them. You can use either a whisk or a rubber spatula. First add a small amount of the mixture you're folding in to the other ingredients. Cut straight down through the center of the mixture to the bottom of the bowl, then turn the whisk or spatula toward you and lift up. Turn the bowl an inch or two, and repeat, working around the bowl just until no streaks remain. Then add the remainder and fold in.

MEASURING FLOUR The way you measure flour for a dessert recipe is crucial to the final outcome. For these recipes, first stir the flour in the canister to aerate it, then spoon it into the measuring cup so that it overflows the cup and level the top with a table knife or other straightedge. Dipping the measuring cup into the flour and scooping it out will give you a different amount of flour, and your results may be disappointing. ANOTHER CAVEAT: 1 cup flour, sifted, is different from 1 cup sifted flour; pay close attention to whether the flour is sifted before or after measuring, or both. Always use metal measuring cups for dry ingredients.

MEASURING BROWN SUGAR Firmly pack the sugar into a metal measuring cup, pressing down on it hard enough so that it will hold its shape when turned out. Use a small metal spatula or a table knife to level off the top.

PREPARING CAKE PANS AND BAKING SHEETS For greased pans, just smear the bottom and sides with softened butter. If a pan also needs to be floured, add a little flour to the pan and shake and turn it so that the sides and bottom are covered with a thin coating. Then turn the pan upside down and gently shake out any excess flour.

ROLLING OUT PASTRY Place the disk of dough on a lightly floured smooth work surface and sprinkle it and the rolling pin with flour. Roll out the dough with short, even strokes, working from the center out, lifting and turning the pastry as you roll. To transfer the dough to the pan, carefully fold it over the rolling pin, lift it up gently, and drape it over the pan. For sticky or hard-to-handle doughs, you can put the disk of dough on a sheet of floured wax paper, flour the dough, and place another sheet of wax paper over the dough before rolling it out. Using wax paper is also good if crusts make you nervous, and you need to build your confidence.

USING A PASTRY BAG AND TIPS For the recipes in this book, you'll need only a good pastry bag with a basic set of tips, if you choose to use one at all. Choose a bag that's a comfortable size for you. To use the bag, insert the appropriate tip, forcing it into the hole at the narrow end of the bag for a snug fit. Then fold the tip end up against the bag to keep what's inside from oozing out while you're filling the bag, place the bag tip-end down in a large glass measuring cup, and fold the edges down around the outside of the cup. Using a rubber spatula, scoop the filling into the bag. Remove the bag from the cup and twist the top closed. Hold the bag firmly with one hand just above its contents, and use the other hand to guide the tip. Gently squeeze the fill-ing, frosting, or other ingredient out with the upper hand. I like disposable plastic bags; the traditional canvas ones can be difficult to clean.

A NOTE ON COOKING TIMES When a range of cooking or baking times is given (for example, "Bake for 30 to 40 minutes"), always check after the first increment of time has elapsed and then continue to watch closely until done.

simple chocolate garnishes

These decorations are easy to prepare, but they all look elegant and very professional and are the perfect finishing touch to your desserts. Any "mistakes" can be melted and the chocolate used again—or nibbled by the cook.

short chocolate curls

Use a large long piece or bar of chocolate—dark, milk, or white—at warm room temperature. Peel curls from the bar with a sharp sturdy vegetable peeler, pressing firmly; the pressure you apply will determine the thickness of the curls. Let the curls fall directly onto the dessert you're garnishing, or drop them onto a sheet of wax paper and refrigerate until ready to use. It's best not to touch the curls with your fingers, as they melt easily; use a paring knife or a wooden pick to move them. These look fabulous piled high on a pudding, cake, or tart. Or just about anything else.

longer chocolate curls

Using a long thin metal spatula, spread melted chocolate evenly over the back of a baking sheet to less than ¼ inch thick. Let stand at room temperature until set. Holding a pancake turner at a forty-five degree angle to the surface of the chocolate, push away from yourself, shaving off long curls. Lift up the curls carefully with a wooden pick or a paring knife to transfer them to the dessert or a sheet of wax paper.

chocolate shavings

Prepare shaved chocolate the same way as choco-late curls, but use short quick strokes of the peeler and a cool piece of chocolate.

grated chocolate

Use a small cool block of chocolate (refrigerate it first for up to 30 minutes if it's a hot day) and brush it against the grater—using any size holes. A standard box grater or a Microplane will do the job.

chocolate cutouts

Line the back of a baking sheet with wax paper. Spread a layer of melted chocolate as thin as possible, between ⅛ and ¼ inch thick. Let stand until almost set, then use cookie cutters, canapé cutters, or a knife point to cut out shapes, leaving them on the sheet. Refrigerate until completely set. Gently break the shapes apart and peel away the wax paper, handling the chocolate as little as possible. Refrigerate until ready to use.

chocolate leaves

Wash and thoroughly dry nonsprayed, nontoxic fresh leaves with well-defined veins, such as lemon or rose. Brush the heavily veined side of each leaf with a thick (at least ⅛ inch), even layer of melted chocolate, leaving a bit of the leaf next to the stem uncoated so it will be easy to remove the chocolate leaf. (Four ounces of chocolate should be enough to cover about 20 leaves.) Lay the leaves on wax paper, and let stand for about 10 minutes, until the chocolate is set. Quickly but carefully pull off the leaves. If not using immediately, transfer the chocolate leaves to a plate and refrigerate, loosely covered.

There are chocolate cakes and then there are all other cakes. As Laurie Colwin so aptly said, "Anyone who spends any time in the kitchen eventually comes to realize that what he or she is looking for is the perfect chocolate cake." If you have a good chocolate cake or two (or the nine here!) in your repertoire, you can conquer any cooking situation and you will always be prepared.

cakes

Here are six supersophisticated cakes—CLASSIC CHOCOLATE POUND CAKE (page 40), CHANTERELLE'S CHOCOLATE SOUFFLÉ CAKE (page 46), INDIVIDUAL MOLTEN CHOCOLATE CAKES (page 35), CHOCOLATE CHIP GINGERBREAD CAKE (page 45), THE ORIGINAL CHOCOLATE DECADENCE (page 42), and MAGNIFICENT MOUSSE CAKE FOR A PARTY (page 38). There is also a very homey MOCHA BROWNIE PUDDING CAKE (page 39), as well as two cakes that are good anytime—LUSCIOUS CHOCOLATE LAYER CAKE (page 32) and everyone's favorite, DIVINE DEVIL'S FOOD CAKE (page 37).

continued

LUSCIOUS CHOCOLATE LAYER CAKE

CAKE

½ cup natural cocoa powder

½ cup boiling water

2¼ cups sifted all-purpose flour

1½ teaspoons baking soda

¼ teaspoon salt

¾ cup (1½ sticks) unsalted butter,
at room temperature

1¾ cups sugar

1 teaspoon pure vanilla extract

2 large eggs

1⅓ cups sour cream

I love the very rich, very chocolatey frosting with this cocoa cake—it's homey and has lots of chocolate flavor. Be sure to use natural cocoa in this recipe, not alkalized or Dutch-process. **SERVES 8 TO 10**

POSITION a rack in the middle of the oven and preheat the oven to 350°F. Butter and flour two 9-by-2-inch round cake pans.

TO MAKE THE CAKE: Whisk together the cocoa and boiling water in a small bowl until smooth. Whisk together the flour, baking soda, and salt in a medium bowl.

BEAT the butter, sugar, and vanilla with an electric mixer on medium speed in a large deep bowl until well blended; the mixture will be dry. Add the eggs one at a time, beating well after each addition. Reduce the speed to low and beat in the flour mixture alternately with the sour cream, beginning and ending with the flour, just until well blended. Add the cocoa mixture and blend well. Divide the batter evenly between the prepared pans.

BAKE for 40 minutes, or until a wooden pick inserted near the center comes out clean. Cool the cakes in the pans on wire racks for 20 minutes, then invert the cakes onto the racks and remove the pans. Turn the cakes right-side up and cool completely.

continued

FROSTING

**6 ounces bittersweet
or semisweet chocolate, chopped**

2 tablespoons water

½ cup sugar

4 large egg yolks

¾ teaspoon pure vanilla extract

**1 cup (2 sticks) unsalted butter,
cut into 16 pieces, at room temperature**

LUSCIOUS CHOCOLATE LAYER CAKE *continued*

TO MAKE THE FROSTING: Melt the chocolate with the water in a small heatproof bowl set over a saucepan of about 1½ inches of nearly simmering water, whisking until smooth. Transfer to a large deep bowl.

HEAT the sugar with the egg yolks in another heatproof bowl over the same saucepan of nearly simmering water, whisking constantly, for about 4 minutes, until the sugar is dissolved and the mixture is warm to the touch. Whisk the sugar mixture into the chocolate mixture, add the vanilla, and beat with an electric mixer on high speed for 3 minutes, or until the mixture has cooled to room temperature. Beat in the butter one piece at a time, beating until smooth after each addition.

TO ASSEMBLE THE CAKE: Place 1 cake layer on a serving plate. Spread about 1 cup of the frosting evenly over the layer. Top with the remaining cake layer and frost with the remaining frosting.

SERVE cut into wedges.

4 ounces bittersweet or semisweet chocolate, chopped

½ cup (1 stick) unsalted butter, cut into pieces

2 large eggs

2 large egg yolks

¼ cup granulated sugar

3 tablespoons all-purpose flour

Confectioners' sugar or unsweetened cocoa powder for dusting

POSITION a rack in the middle of the oven and preheat the oven to 450°F. Butter and flour four 4-ounce ramekins or 6-ounce custard cups, then butter and flour them again.

MELT the chocolate with the butter in a heatproof bowl set over a saucepan of about 1½ inches of nearly simmering water, whisking until smooth. Remove the bowl from the heat.

INDIVIDUAL MOLTEN CHOCOLATE CAKES

First served at Layfayette restaurant when Jean-George Vongerichten was chef in the late 1980s, this chocolate cake has been the most copied dessert in New York City restaurants—and beyond—for years. And with good reason. This luscious soft cake looks conventional on the plate, but when you cut into it, the center is runny, like the yolk of a soft-boiled egg (Jean-George says it was an accident). It's wonderful served with caramel, coffee, or vanilla ice cream. **SERVES 4**

MEANWHILE, beat the eggs, yolks, and granulated sugar with an electric mixer on high speed in a medium deep bowl for about 8 minutes, until very thick and pale. Whisk in the warm chocolate mixture, then whisk in the flour just until blended.

DIVIDE the batter evenly among the ramekins. Arrange the ramekins on a baking sheet and bake for 14 minutes, or until the cakes have risen and have a thin crust, their sides are set, and they are still slightly jiggly at the center; underbaking is better than overbaking.

CAREFULLY invert each ramekin onto a serving plate and let sit for 20 seconds, then unmold by lifting up one side of the ramekin; the cake will fall onto the plate. Dust the tops with confectioners' sugar.

SERVE immediately.

POSITION a rack in the middle of the oven and preheat the oven to 350°F. Butter two 9-by-2-inch round cake pans, line the bottoms with aluminum foil, and butter the foil.

CAKE

2 cups cake flour (not self-rising)

⅔ cup natural cocoa powder

1¼ teaspoons baking soda

¼ teaspoon salt

½ cup buttermilk

⅓ cup water

¾ cup (1½ sticks) unsalted butter, at room temperature

1¾ cups sugar

2 large eggs

1½ teaspoons pure vanilla extract

TO MAKE THE CAKE: Sift together the flour, cocoa powder, baking soda, and salt into a large bowl. Stir together the buttermilk and water in a small bowl.

BEAT the butter with an electric mixer on medium-high speed in a large bowl until light and fluffy. Add the sugar and beat for 3 minutes, or until light and fluffy. Add the eggs one at a time, beating well after each addition. Beat in the vanilla. Reduce the speed to low and add the cocoa mixture alternately with the buttermilk mixture in 3 batches, beating just until well blended. Transfer the batter to the pans and smooth the tops with a rubber spatula.

BAKE for 35 minutes, or until a wooden pick inserted into the center comes out clean. Cool the cakes in the pans on wire racks for 5 minutes. Carefully invert onto the racks, turn right-side up, and let cool completely. Remove the foil.

DIVINE DEVIL'S FOOD CAKE

Dark and dense, this is. You might also make this as cupcakes—it will make 24 and you may have a little icing left over.

SERVES 8

FROSTING

7½ ounces bittersweet or semisweet chocolate, chopped

½ cup heavy (whipping) cream

3 tablespoons unsalted butter, at room temperature

TO MAKE THE FROSTING: Melt the chocolate with the cream in a heatproof medium deep bowl set over a saucepan of about 1½ inches of nearly simmering water, whisking until smooth. Add the butter and whisk until smooth. Let cool to room temperature, then refrigerate, covered, for 15 minutes.

BEAT the frosting with an electric mixer on medium-high speed for about 8 minutes, until thick enough to spread.

TO ASSEMBLE THE CAKE: Place 1 cake layer on a serving plate. Spread about 1 cup of the frosting evenly over the layer. Top with the remaining cake layer and frost the top and sides with the remaining frosting. Refrigerate for at least 1 hour, until the frosting sets.

SERVE cut into wedges.

POSITION a rack in the middle of the oven and preheat the oven to 300°F. Butter a 9-inch springform pan.

1 pound bittersweet or semisweet chocolate, chopped

MELT the chocolate with the butter in a heatproof bowl set over a saucepan of about 1½ inches of nearly simmering water, whisking until smooth. Remove the bowl from the heat and set aside.

1 pound unsalted butter, cut into pieces, at room temperature

7 large eggs, separated

7 large egg yolks

¾ cup superfine sugar

2 teaspoons pure vanilla extract

¼ teaspoon salt

WHISK together the 14 egg yolks and sugar in a large heatproof bowl. Place the bowl over the same saucepan of nearly simmering water and whisk for about 3 minutes, until the sugar is dissolved and the mixture is warm to the touch. Remove the bowl from the heat and beat the mixture with an electric mixer on medium-high speed for about 4 minutes, until it has cooled to room temperature and is very thick and pale. Whisk in the chocolate mixture in 3 batches, just until well blended. Whisk in the vanilla.

MAGNIFICENT MOUSSE CAKE FOR A PARTY

You'll love this—it's *sooo* easy, very clever, and incredibly urbane. All you do is make a batter with lots of good chocolate, butter, and eggs (and I mean lots—look at the ingredient list!) and bake most of it, then use the remaining batter as a frosting after the cake has cooled. Pretty clever! **SERVES 12 TO 16**

BEAT the egg whites and salt with clean beaters on medium-high speed in a large deep bowl until the whites form soft peaks when the beaters are lifted. Gently whisk the egg whites into the chocolate mixture in 3 batches. Transfer 2 cups of the batter to a bowl, cover, and set aside.

POUR the remaining batter into the prepared pan. Bake for 40 to 50 minutes, until a wooden pick inserted in the center comes out sticky but not wet; the top will be cracked. Let cool completely in the pan on a wire rack; the center will sink.

REMOVE the sides of the pan. Fill the fallen center of the cake with the remaining chocolate mixture and smooth the top. Refrigerate, loosely covered, until thoroughly chilled, at least 2 hours, or up to 1 day.

ABOUT 1 hour before serving, remove the cake from the refrigerator. Serve cut into thin wedges.

NOTE: You can make your own superfine sugar in the food processor by pulsing granulated sugar until it is very finely ground.

I cup all-purpose flour

1¼ cups packed dark brown sugar

6 tablespoons Dutch-process
cocoa powder

2 teaspoons baking powder

¼ teaspoon salt

½ cup whole milk

3 tablespoons unsalted butter, melted

2 teaspoons pure vanilla extract

2 tablespoons cocoa nibs (optional)

1½ cups very hot brewed coffee

Slightly sweetened whipped cream or
vanilla ice cream for serving (optional)

POSITION a rack in the middle of the oven and preheat the oven to 350°F. Butter an 8-inch square baking pan.

WHISK together the flour, ¾ cup of the sugar, 2 tablespoons of the cocoa, the baking powder, and salt in a medium bowl; breaking up any large lumps of sugar with your hands. Stir in the milk, butter, and vanilla with a wooden spoon just until blended; the batter will be very thick. Transfer to the baking dish and smooth the top with a rubber spatula.

STIR together the remaining ½ cup sugar and ¼ cup cocoa with a fork in a small bowl; breaking up any large lumps of sugar with your hands. Stir in the nibs, if using. Sprinkle the mixture evenly over the batter. Pour the hot coffee evenly over the batter—do not stir.

MOCHA BROWNIE PUDDING CAKE

This recipe may look as if it has a lot of ingredients, but it takes just minutes to put together. The result is the best of all possible worlds—brownies with their own pudding. It is best served hot or warm; if necessary, you can gently rewarm it in the oven or microwave just before serving. Because the recipe uses baking powder, be sure to use Dutch-process cocoa. You don't have to use the nibs, but you SHOULD. **SERVES 6 TO 8**

BAKE for 30 to 35 minutes, until the top layer is set and the dessert is beginning to pull away from the sides of the pan; the batter will have separated into cake and pudding layers. Cool in the pan on a wire rack for at least 15 minutes.

SERVE hot, warm, or at room temperature in small bowls, with whipped cream, if desired.

I cup sifted cake flour (not self-rising)

¼ cup finely ground almonds

4 ounces bittersweet or semisweet chocolate, chopped

5 tablespoons water

½ cup (I stick) unsalted butter, at room temperature

½ cup sugar

2 large eggs, separated

I large egg white

¼ teaspoon salt

Slightly sweetened whipped cream or crème fraîche for serving (optional)

POSITION a rack in the middle of the oven and preheat the oven to 325°F. Butter and flour a 7-inch (5 cup) Kugelhopf pan or Bundt pan. Have a roasting pan ready, and put a kettle of water on to boil for the water bath.

SIFT the flour into a medium bowl, and stir in the ground almonds.

MELT the chocolate with the water in a heatproof bowl set over a saucepan of about 1½ inches of nearly simmering water, whisking until smooth. Remove the bowl from the heat and set aside.

BEAT the butter and sugar with an electric mixer on medium-high speed in a large deep bowl for about 4 minutes, until light and fluffy. Beat in the egg yolks one at a time, beating well after each addition. Add the chocolate mixture and beat just until well blended. Reduce the speed to low and add the flour mixture in 2 batches, scraping down the sides of the bowl as necessary and beating just until blended.

CLASSIC CHOCOLATE POUND CAKE

This stunning recipe is adapted from one by Sally Darr that I worked on when I was at *Gourmet* magazine. She had adapted it from a recipe in Ferdinand Point's classic book, *Ma Gastronomie*. He got it from his neighbor, Juliette—and now it's yours. It's an unusual pound cake, baked in a water bath and made with chocolate rather than cocoa. It's so good it doesn't need adornment—well, maybe just a drizzle of CREAMY CHOCO-LATE SAUCE (page 136). **SERVES 8**

BEAT the egg whites and salt with clean beaters on medium-high speed in a large bowl just until the whites form stiff peaks when the beaters are lifted. With a whisk or a rubber spatula, fold one-quarter of the whites into the chocolate mixture to lighten it, then fold in the remaining whites. Transfer the batter to the cake pan and smooth the top. Place the roasting pan in the oven, put the cake pan in it, and add enough hot water to reach halfway up the sides of the cake pan.

BAKE for 1¼ hours, or until a wooden pick inserted in the center comes out clean. Remove the cake pan from the water bath and let the cake cool in the pan on a wire rack for 10 minutes. Turn the cake out onto the rack and let cool completely.

SERVE cut into wedges, with whipped cream, if desired.

1 pound bittersweet or
semisweet chocolate, chopped

½ cup (1 stick) plus 2 tablespoons
unsalted butter

4 large eggs

1 tablespoon granulated sugar

1 tablespoon all-purpose flour

2 cups heavy (whipping) cream

1 tablespoon confectioners' sugar

1 teaspoon pure vanilla extract

CHOCOLATE CURLS for garnish
(see page 28)

RASPBERRY SAUCE (page 138)

POSITION a rack in the middle of the oven and preheat the oven to 425°F. Butter an 8-by-2-inch round cake pan and line the pan with parchment paper.

MELT the chocolate with the butter in a heatproof bowl set over a saucepan of about 1½ inches of nearly simmering water, whisking until smooth. Remove the bowl from the heat and set aside.

THE ORIGINAL CHOCOLATE DECADENCE

This dessert changed my life. It was invented by Janet Feuer, the pastry chef at Narsai's restaurant in north Berkeley in the early 1970s. It was a revelation, because I had no idea a dessert could be so rich and have such intense chocolate flavor. Janet wrote a book about the recipe, and it's the only cookbook I've ever seen containing just one recipe. Narsai added the raspberry sauce.

HEAT the eggs with the sugar in a large heatproof bowl over the same saucepan of nearly simmering water, whisking constantly, for about 4 minutes, until the sugar is dissolved and the mixture is warm to the touch. Remove the bowl from the heat and beat the mixture with an electric mixer on medium-high speed for about 4 minutes, until it is very thick and pale. Fold in the flour with a whisk or a rubber spatula.

WHISK one-third of the egg mixture into the chocolate mixture. Fold the chocolate mixture into the remaining egg mixture just until no longer marbled. Transfer the batter to the pan and tap the pan lightly on the counter to remove any air bubbles.

BAKE for about 15 minutes, until the cake is set around the edges but still jiggly in the center; do not overbake. Let cool to room temperature in the pan on a wire rack.

WRAP the cake tightly in aluminum foil and freeze for at least 12 hours. (The cake can be frozen for up to 1 month.)

You could make this with just 1 cup of cream for the frosting instead of the 2 cups called for in the original recipe; I think it's plenty. (Remember to halve the sugar and vanilla, too.) Use up to one-quarter pound of chocolate for the chocolate curls.

SERVES 12

ABOUT 15 minutes before serving, unwrap the cake pan and spin the pan on a burner over high heat for a few seconds to release the frozen cake from the pan. Run a table knife around the edges of the pan to loosen the cake, place a serving platter over the pan, and invert the pan onto it. Lift off the pan and discard the parchment paper.

WHIP the cream with an electric mixer on medium-high speed in a large bowl just until it forms soft peaks when the beaters are lifted. Add the confectioners' sugar and vanilla and whip just until the cream forms stiff peaks when the beaters are lifted. Cover the top and sides of the cake with two-thirds of the whipped cream. Pile the chocolate curls in the center, and pipe the remaining whipped cream around the edge of the cake, using a star tip. Refrigerate until 15 minutes before serving.

SERVE cut into wedges, with the Raspberry Sauce.

2½ cups, plus 2 tablespoons all-purpose flour

½ cup natural cocoa powder, plus additional for dusting

1 teaspoon baking soda

½ teaspoon salt

1½ teaspoons ground ginger

1 teaspoon ground cinnamon

½ teaspoon ground allspice

¼ teaspoon ground cloves

¼ teaspoon ground nutmeg

¼ teaspoon freshly ground black pepper

The lovely Rosanne Toroian at *Good Housekeeping* magazine devised this gingerbread cake, and I thought it was the best one I had ever tasted. But, of course, I decided to add some chocolate chips. I think you'll like it. Don't be intimidated—it may look like lots of ingredients, but it's mostly spices that can be measured very quickly. Make sure to use natural cocoa powder. **SERVES 12**

POSITION a rack in the middle of the oven and preheat the oven to 350°F. Butter and flour a 10-cup Bundt pan.

WHISK together 2½ cups of the flour, the ½ cup cocoa, baking soda, salt, ginger, cinnamon, allspice, cloves, nutmeg, and pepper in a medium bowl.

CHOCOLATE CHIP GINGERBREAD CAKE

One 12-ounce package miniature semisweet chocolate chips

¾ cup (1½ sticks) unsalted butter, at room temperature

1¼ cups sugar

1 teaspoon pure vanilla extract

2 large eggs

1 cup dark molasses

1 cup very hot water

TOSS the chocolate chips with the remaining 2 tablespoons flour in another medium bowl.

BEAT the butter, sugar, and vanilla with an electric mixer on medium-high speed in a large deep bowl, occasionally scraping down the sides of the bowl with a rubber spatula, for about 3 minutes, until light and fluffy. Reduce the speed to medium and add the eggs one at a time, beating well after each addition.

WHISK together the molasses and hot water in a 4-cup glass measure or a bowl. Reduce the mixer speed to low and add the flour mixture alternately with the molasses mixture in 3 batches, occasionally scraping down the sides of the bowl with the spatula and beating just until well blended. Fold in the chocolate chips.

TRANSFER the batter to the prepared pan. Bake for 55 to 60 minutes, until the cake begins to pull away from the sides of the pan and is firm to the touch. Cool the cake in the pan on a wire rack for 20 minutes. Invert the cake onto the rack and cool completely.

SERVE, lightly dusted with cocoa, and cut into wedges.

POSITION a rack in the middle of the oven and preheat the oven to 300°F. Butter and flour a 9-inch springform pan and line the bottom with parchment paper.

MELT the chocolate with the butter in a heatproof bowl set over a saucepan of about 1½ inches of nearly simmering water, whisking until smooth. Remove the bowl from the heat and let cool to room temperature.

BEAT the egg yolks and ¾ cup of the sugar with an electric mixer on medium-high speed in a large deep bowl for 4 to 5 minutes, until very thick and pale.

BEAT the egg whites with clean beaters in another large bowl just until the whites form soft peaks when the beaters are lifted. Beat in the remaining 1 tablespoon sugar.

I pound bittersweet or semisweet chocolate, chopped

I cup (2 sticks) unsalted butter

9 large eggs, separated

¾ cup, plus I tablespoon sugar

Unsweetened cocoa powder for dusting

Confectioners' sugar for dusting

CHANTERELLE'S CHOCOLATE SOUFFLÉ CAKE

This recipe is adapted from the wonderful book *Staff Meals from Chanterelle*, recipes for the staff meals served at one of the world's best restaurants, in downtown Manhattan. It is totally chocolate and very easy to make. And it's topped with alternating layers of cocoa powder and confectioners' sugar, a garnish you might want to use on other chocolate desserts— it's simple but stunning.

SERVES 10 TO 12

WITH a whisk or a rubber spatula, gently fold one-third of the cooled chocolate mixture into the egg yolk mixture. Then fold in one-third of the egg whites. Repeat, adding the chocolate and egg white mixtures alternately in thirds until all of the ingredients are combined.

TRANSFER the batter to the prepared pan. Bake for about 30 minutes, until the edges are firm and the center is puffed but still a bit jiggly; do not overbake. Transfer to a wire rack to cool completely.

TO SERVE, remove the sides of the pan. Dust the cake with a layer of cocoa and then with a layer of confectioners' sugar. Repeat with a second layer of cocoa and a final layer of sugar. Cut into thin wedges.

There are some of us who prefer a pie, tart, or cheesecake to a birthday cake. If you favor them, think of these pies, tarts, and cheesecake as your future birthday cakes! Begin with the **QUICKEST, EASIEST CHOCOLATE MOUSSE PIE** (page 65), because if you're going to make your own birthday pie, it had better be easy. But don't worry about it being good enough—it will be tremendous. And don't worry about it being chocolatey enough—it will be. The **DEEP DARK CHOCOLATE CREAM PIE** (page 52), with or without the Mascarpone Topping, is rich and wonderful and totally chocolate—and birthday candles look great in it.

pies + tarts + a cheesecake

If cheesecake is your thing, whip up the **KILLER CHOCOLATE CHEESECAKE** (page 63). You'll be very proud of yourself. There is almost nothing more elegant than a chocolate tart, so give the **PERFECTLY SIMPLE DARK CHOCO- LATE TART** (page 51) a try. You'll be very pleased with the results: it will look just like something from a fancy pastry shop. The **BROWNIE PIE** (page 60) and **CHOCOLATE PECAN TURTLE TART** (page 54) are crowd-pleasers and will make everyone very happy. Or, at least, whip up my **MOM'S CHOCOLATE ANGEL PIE—AND THEN SOME** (page 57), and savor the celebration of textures.

POSITION a rack in the middle of the oven and preheat the oven to 350°F. Lightly butter an 11-inch fluted tart pan with a removable bottom.

TO MAKE THE CRUST: Process the sugar and walnuts in a food processor until the walnuts are finely ground. Add the flour, cocoa, and salt and pulse just until blended. Add the butter and pulse just until the mixture begins to come together when a small amount is pressed between your fingers; do not overprocess—the mixture should not form a ball. Press the dough evenly into the bottom and up the sides of the tart pan. Prick the dough all over with a fork.

BAKE for 15 to 18 minutes, until the crust begins to pull away from the sides of the pan. Let cool on a wire rack while you make the filling.

CRUST

½ cup confectioners' sugar

¼ cup toasted walnuts, cooled

¾ cup all-purpose flour

¼ cup unsweetened cocoa powder

¼ teaspoon salt

½ cup (1 stick) cold unsalted butter, cut into small pieces

PERFECTLY SIMPLE DARK CHOCOLATE TART

Parisian in spirit, this elegant tart is great served with a tiny dollop of crème fraîche on the top or side of each wedge. **SERVES 12**

TO MAKE THE FILLING: Melt the chocolate with the butter in a heatproof bowl set over a saucepan of about 1½ inches of nearly simmering water, whisking until smooth. Remove the bowl from the heat and whisk in the eggs and sugar until well blended. Whisk in the vanilla. Transfer the filling to the warm crust.

BAKE for about 12 minutes, until the filling is set around the edges but still slightly jiggly in the center; the top of the tart will look a little blistered, and that's okay. Transfer to a wire rack to cool completely, at least 1½ hours.

TO SERVE, remove the pan rim. Lightly dust the tart with cocoa powder and cut into wedges.

FILLING

14 ounces bittersweet or semisweet chocolate, chopped

6 tablespoons unsalted butter

2 large eggs, lightly beaten

¼ cup sugar

1 teaspoon pure vanilla extract

Cocoa powder for dusting

DEEP DARK CHOCOLATE CREAM PIE

Not that you can't serve this as is—you can and you'll be very happy—but you have a couple of other options. You can serve it with whipped cream instead of the mascarpone topping, either on the side or dolloped on top, or piped on top in rosettes with a star tip, or simply spread over the top of the pie to cover it completely. **SERVES 8**

CRUST

1 cup plus 2 tablespoons all-purpose flour

1½ teaspoons sugar

¼ teaspoon salt

6 tablespoons (¾ stick) cold unsalted butter, cut into small pieces

2 tablespoons cold whole milk

1½ teaspoons distilled white vinegar

TO MAKE THE CRUST: Whisk together the flour, sugar, and salt in a medium bowl. Cut in the butter with a pastry blender or 2 knives used scissors-fashion until the butter is the size of small peas. Add the milk and vinegar and stir with a fork just until the dough begins to come together when a small bit is pressed between your fingers; do not overwork the dough. Press the dough together to form a ball and knead lightly. Shape the dough into a disk and chill, wrapped in wax paper, for at least 30 minutes, or up to 2 days.

POSITION a rack in the bottom third of the oven and preheat the oven to 400°F. Have a 9-inch glass pie plate ready.

ROLL out the dough on a lightly floured surface or between 2 sheets of wax paper to an 11-inch circle. Transfer the dough to the pie plate and gently press the pastry against the bottom and sides of the plate. Turn the edge under and crimp as desired. Line the shell with a piece of heavy-duty aluminum foil, pressing it snugly into the bottom and against the sides of the pastry shell, and fill with uncooked rice or beans.

BAKE the crust for 12 minutes. Remove the foil and rice and bake for 7 minutes longer, or until golden brown. Let cool to room temperature on a wire rack.

FILLING

2 cups whole milk

I cup heavy (whipping) cream

I cup sugar

2 large eggs

4 large egg yolks

3 tablespoons cornstarch

2 tablespoons unsweetened cocoa powder

¼ teaspoon salt

8 ounces bittersweet or semisweet chocolate, finely chopped

I teaspoon pure vanilla extract

TO MAKE THE FILLING: Bring 1½ cups of the milk, the cream, and sugar just to a boil in a large saucepan over medium heat, whisking until the sugar is dissolved. Remove the pan from the heat. Whisk together the eggs, yolks, cornstarch, cocoa, salt, and the remaining ½ cup milk in a medium bowl until smooth. Whisking constantly, slowly pour the milk mixture into the egg mixture, whisking until smooth. Return to the saucepan and bring to a boil over medium-low heat, whisking constantly. Boil for 1 minute. Remove the pan from the heat and whisk in the chocolate. Whisk until smooth.

POUR the filling through a coarse strainer into a bowl and let cool, whisking frequently, to room temperature. Whisk in the vanilla.

TOPPING

I cup mascarpone cheese

I cup heavy (whipping) cream

¼ cup sugar

½ teaspoon pure vanilla extract

TO MAKE THE TOPPING: Whip together the mascarpone, heavy cream, sugar, and vanilla in a large bowl until stiff peaks form when the beaters are lifted.

TRANSFER the filling to the pie shell and smooth the top with a rubber spatula. Spread the topping over the filling. Cover the pie loosely and refrigerate for at least 2 hours, or up to 1 day.

SERVE the pie chilled, cut into wedges.

CRUST

1 cup all-purpose flour

⅓ cup unsweetened cocoa powder

2 tablespoons sugar

¼ teaspoon salt

½ cup (1 stick) cold unsalted butter, cut into small pieces

2 to 3 tablespoons ice water

continued

TO MAKE THE CRUST: Whisk together the flour, cocoa, sugar, and salt in a medium bowl. Cut in the butter with a pastry blender or 2 knives used scissors-fashion until the butter is the size of small peas. Sprinkle 1 tablespoon of the water over the flour mixture, stirring gently with a fork to distribute the moisture evenly. Continue adding water until the dough just begins to come together when a small bit is pressed between your fingers; do not overwork the dough. Press the dough together to form a ball and knead slightly. Shape into a disk and chill, wrapped in wax paper, for at least 30 minutes, or up to 2 days.

POSITION a rack in the middle of the oven and preheat the oven to 425°F. Have a 9-inch fluted tart pan with a removable bottom ready.

CHOCOLATE PECAN TURTLE TART

My friend Judith Sutton is a true chocolate lover. She does many things very well, and one of my favorites of all her efforts is this tart. If you don't have a pastry bag, or don't want to use one, just dollop the whipped cream on the side or on top of each serving. **SERVES 10 TO 12**

ROLL out the dough between 2 sheets of wax paper to a 12½-inch round. Peel off the top sheet of wax paper. Transfer the dough to the tart pan, wax-paper-side up, and gently press the pastry against the bottom and sides; peel off the paper. Line the shell with a piece of heavy-duty aluminum foil, pressing it snugly into the bottom and against the sides of the shell, and fill with uncooked rice or beans.

BAKE the shell for 15 minutes. Remove the foil and the rice and bake for 8 minutes longer, or until lightly browned. Let cool to room temperature on a wire rack.

continued

FILLING

2 cups heavy (whipping) cream

3 ½ ounces bittersweet or semisweet chocolate, finely chopped

½ teaspoon pure vanilla extract

2 ¼ cups sugar

¾ cup water

1 ½ tablespoons light corn syrup

1 ¼ cups toasted pecan halves, plus 8 toasted pecan halves for garnish

TO MAKE THE FILLING: Bring ¾ cup of the cream just to a boil in a medium saucepan over medium-high heat. Remove the pan from the heat, add the chocolate, and whisk until smooth. Let cool to room temperature, then whisk in the vanilla. Refrigerate, covered, for 1 hour, or until cold.

MEANWHILE, bring the sugar, water, and corn syrup to a boil in a medium heavy saucepan over medium-high heat, stirring until the sugar dissolves. Boil, without stirring, brushing down the sides of the pan with a damp pastry brush if you see sugar crystals forming, for about 15 minutes, until dark golden brown. Reduce the heat to low, carefully pour in ¾ cup of the cream, and stir until smooth. Stir in the 1 ¼ cups pecans.

CHOCOLATE PECAN TURTLE TART *continued*

TRANSFER the caramel mixture to the tart shell and let cool to room temperature, then refrigerate for about 20 minutes, until firm.

BEAT the cold chocolate mixture with an electric mixer on low speed for about 1 minute, just until it forms soft peaks when the beaters are lifted. Spread the chocolate mixture over the caramel. (The tart can be made ahead to this point and refrigerated, covered, for up to 3 days.)

TO SERVE, whip the remaining ½ cup cream with an electric mixer on medium-high speed in a medium bowl just until stiff peaks form when the beaters are lifted. Pipe 8 rosettes around the edge of the tart and decorate with the 8 pecan halves. Cut into wedges.

MERINGUE SHELL

**4 large egg whites,
at room temperature**

¼ teaspoon cream of tartar

Pinch of salt

I cup granulated sugar

continued

POSITION a rack in the middle of the oven and preheat the oven to 225°F. Trace a 9-inch circle on a sheet of parchment paper. Place the paper on a baking sheet, turning it upside down so the pencil marking faces down.

TO MAKE THE SHELL: Beat the egg whites with an electric mixer on medium speed in a large bowl until foamy. Increase the speed to medium-high, add the cream of tartar and salt, and beat just until the egg whites form soft peaks when the beaters are lifted. Add the sugar about I tablespoon at a time, and beat just until the whites form stiff peaks when the beaters are lifted.

MOM'S CHOCOLATE ANGEL PIE—AND THEN SOME

My mom often served this, one of my childhood favorites, for a special dinner. She got the recipe from one of the *Ladies' Home Journal* cookbooks, and I've changed it over the years because I just couldn't help myself. I've added more chocolate and I used lots of fresh berries for a topping. The combination of the crisp meringue shell and the smooth and creamy chocolate filling, topped with cool berries is a winner. *continued*

SPOON the meringue into a pastry bag fitted with a large star tip. Starting at the outside edge, pipe the meringue in a spiral to fill the traced circle on the parchment. Holding the pastry bag upright and starting at the outer edge, pipe a ring of rosettes along the edge for the rim, then pipe a second tier of rosettes on the shoulders of the first tier. Or, if you don't have a pastry bag, spoon the meringue into the circle, scooping the sides upward to form a rim.

BAKE for I hour, or until the meringue is dry to the touch. Turn off the oven and leave the meringue in the oven for 2 hours. Peel off the paper. (The meringue can be stored, tightly wrapped, for up to I day.)

continued

FILLING

7 ounces bittersweet or semisweet
chocolate, chopped

¼ cup water

I teaspoon pure vanilla extract

I ¼ cups heavy (whipping) cream

2 cups mixed fresh berries

Confectioners' sugar and/or
unsweetened cocoa powder for dusting

MOM'S CHOCOLATE ANGEL PIE—AND THEN SOME *continued*

If you'd like, add ½ cup or so of chopped toasted pecans or hazelnuts to the meringue—but only if you are planning to spoon it, as they would jam the pastry tip. You could also add some pitted fresh cherries to the berries. **SERVES 6 TO 8**

ABOUT AN HOUR BEFORE SERVING, MAKE THE FILLING: Melt the chocolate with the water in a heatproof bowl set over a saucepan of about 1½ inches of nearly simmering water, whisking until smooth. Remove the bowl from the heat and let cool to room temperature.

WHISK the vanilla into the cool chocolate and set aside. Beat the cream with an electric mixer on medium-high speed in a large deep bowl just until the cream forms soft peaks when the beaters are lifted. With a whisk or rubber spatula, fold the chocolate mixture into the whipped cream in 3 batches. Transfer the filling to the shell and smooth the top with a rubber spatula. Chill until ready to serve.

TO SERVE, arrange the berries on top of the pie and lightly sift confectioners' sugar over them.

CRUST

1¼ cups all-purpose flour

1 tablespoon sugar

¼ teaspoon salt

6 tablespoons (¾ stick) cold
unsalted butter, cut into small pieces

3 to 4 tablespoons ice water

TO MAKE THE CRUST: Whisk together the flour, sugar, and salt in a medium bowl. Cut in the butter with a pastry blender or 2 knives used scissors-fashion until the butter is the size of small peas. Sprinkle 1 tablespoon of the water over the mixture, stirring gently with a fork to distribute the moisture evenly. Continue adding water just until the dough begins to come together when a small bit is pressed between your fingers; do not overwork the dough. Press the dough together to form a ball and knead lightly. Shape the dough into a disk and chill, wrapped in wax paper, for at least 30 minutes, or up to 2 days.

BROWNIE PIE

Think of these as brownies inside a buttery crisp pastry crust. What could be better? Just add ice cream and a chocolate sauce and you'll have a brownie sundae *and* pie à la mode. Try **LUSCIOUS CHOCOLATE CUSTARD ICE CREAM** (page 118). **SERVES 8**

POSITION a rack in the middle of the oven and preheat the oven to 425°F. Have a 9-inch glass pie plate ready.

ROLL out the dough on a lightly floured surface or between 2 sheets of wax paper to a 12- to 13-inch round. Transfer the dough to the pie plate and gently press the pastry against the bottom and sides of the plate. Turn the edges under and crimp as desired. Line the shell with a piece of heavy-duty aluminum foil, pressing it snugly into the bottom and against the sides, and fill with uncooked rice or beans.

BAKE the crust for 12 minutes. Remove the foil and rice and bake for 4 minutes longer, or until light golden brown. Let cool on a wire rack. Reduce the oven temperature to 350°F.

FILLING

6 ounces bittersweet or semisweet chocolate, chopped

½ cup (1 stick) unsalted butter

3 large eggs

¾ cup sugar

1 teaspoon pure vanilla extract

1 tablespoon unsweetened cocoa powder

½ cup toasted walnuts, chopped

TO MAKE THE FILLING: Melt the chocolate with the butter in a heatproof bowl set over a saucepan of about 1½ inches of nearly simmering water, whisking until smooth. Remove the bowl from the heat and set aside.

BEAT the eggs and sugar with an electric mixer on medium-high speed in a large deep bowl for 4 minutes, or until thick and pale. Beat in the vanilla. Sprinkle the cocoa powder over the mixture and fold in with a whisk or a rubber spatula just until thoroughly blended. Fold in the chocolate mixture and the walnuts. Transfer the batter to the baked crust.

BAKE for 40 to 45 minutes, until a wooden pick inserted in the center comes out slightly sticky, with just a few crumbs clinging to it, but is not wet. Let cool completely on a wire rack.

SERVE cut into wedges.

CRUST

One 9-ounce package chocolate wafers, broken into large pieces

6 tablespoons unsalted butter, melted

continued

KILLER CHOCOLATE CHEESECAKE

Gorgeous and tall, this is a beautiful, bountiful, and glamorous dessert. Be sure to present it in its full glory before cutting it into serving pieces. **SERVES 12**

POSITION a rack in the middle of the oven and preheat the oven to 350°F. Butter a 9-inch springform pan and wrap the outside tightly with heavy-duty aluminum foil. Have a roasting pan ready, and put a kettle of water on to boil for the water bath.

TO MAKE THE CRUST: Pulse the chocolate wafers in a food processor until finely ground. With the motor running, slowly add the butter, and process just until blended. Press the mixture onto the bottom of the pan.

BAKE the crust for 8 to 10 minutes, until it is set. Let cool on a wire rack.

continued

I pound bittersweet or
semisweet chocolate, chopped

¼ cup (½ stick) unsalted butter

2 tablespoons unsweetened cocoa powder

Three 8-ounce packages
cream cheese, at room temperature

I cup sugar

4 large eggs

Pinch of salt

1½ cups sour cream,
at room temperature

2 teaspoons pure vanilla extract

TO MAKE THE FILLING: Melt the chocolate with the butter in a heatproof bowl set over a saucepan of about 1½ inches of nearly simmering water, whisking until smooth. Whisk in the cocoa powder. Remove the bowl from the heat and let the mixture cool to room temperature.

BEAT the cream cheese and sugar with an electric mixer, beginning on low speed and increasing to medium-high, in a medium deep bowl until light and fluffy. Add the eggs one at a time, beating well after each addition. Beat in the salt. Beat in the chocolate mixture just until smooth, scraping down the sides of the bowl with a rubber spatula as necessary. Add the sour cream and vanilla and beat until smooth, scraping down the sides of the bowl again.

KILLER CHOCOLATE CHEESECAKE *continued*

TRANSFER the filling to the springform pan. Set the pan in the roasting pan, place it in the oven, and carefully pour in enough boiling water to reach halfway up the sides of the springform pan. Bake for 45 minutes, or until the center is almost set but still slightly jiggly; do not overbake—the cheesecake will firm as it cools. Remove the roasting pan from the oven and let the cheesecake cool in the water bath for 15 minutes.

REMOVE the springform pan from the water bath and let cool completely on a wire rack, then remove the foil and refrigerate the cheesecake, loosely covered, until thoroughly chilled, at least 12 hours, or overnight.

TO SERVE, let the cheesecake stand at room temperature for 20 minutes. Remove the pan sides, smooth the sides of the cheesecake with a table knife, and cut into wedges.

One 9-ounce package chocolate wafers,
broken into large pieces

6 tablespoons (¾ stick)
unsalted butter, melted

7 ounces bittersweet or semisweet
chocolate, chopped

½ cup strong brewed coffee

1¼ cups heavy (whipping) cream

I teaspoon pure vanilla extract

Pinch of salt

BUTTER a 9-inch springform pan. Pulse the chocolate wafers in a food processor until finely ground. With the motor running, slowly add the butter, and process just until blended. Press the mixture onto the bottom and one-third of the way up the sides of the prepared pan.

MELT the chocolate with the coffee in a heatproof bowl set over a saucepan of about 1½ inches of nearly simmering water, whisking until smooth. Remove the bowl from the heat and let cool for 5 minutes.

QUICKEST, EASIEST CHOCOLATE MOUSSE PIE

Adding coffee (or instant espresso powder) to a recipe can really boost the chocolate flavor; it both enhances and deepens its intensity, as you will see here. Perfect for a party, this pie couldn't be easier to put together or more dramatic to present. **SERVES 8**

WHIP the cream, vanilla, and salt with an electric mixer on medium-high speed in a large deep bowl just until the cream holds stiff peaks when the beaters are lifted. With a whisk or a rubber spatula, fold the chocolate mixture into the cream in 3 batches, just until well blended. Transfer the mousse to the pan and smooth the top with a rubber spatula.

REFRIGERATE, covered, until thoroughly chilled, at least 3 hours, or up to I day.

TO SERVE remove the sides of the pan and cut into wedges.

3

chocolate special favorites

Here's a small, well-chosen, fun collection of special treats. Included are two European classics, **LUSCIOUS CHOCOLATE FONDUE** (page 68), and **CHOCOLATE PROFITEROLES WITH CHOCOLATE ICE CREAM AND CHOCOLATE SAUCE** (page 72), as well as a childhood favorite, **CHOCOLATE WAFER ICEBOX CAKE** (page 74). Speaking of childhood favorites, there is also my summer-camp delight, **GRILLED CHOCOLATE-STUFFED BANANAS** (page 75). There are also a couple of less conventional chocolate desserts that feature the remarkable and timeless combination of chocolate and bread: **HOT CHOCOLATE SAUCE WITH CROUTONS** (page 69) and **CHOCOLATE-HAZELNUT SPREAD ON TOAST WITH NECTARINES** (page 71). Yum.

1 cup heavy (whipping) cream
or crème fraîche

2 tablespoons water

10 ounces bittersweet or semisweet
chocolate, finely chopped

Pinch of salt

1 to 3 tablespoons Cognac or
other brandy, rum, or liqueur (optional)

Brioche, soft crusty country bread,
or baguette, cut into 1-inch cubes

Fresh fruit (see NOTE)

BRING the cream and water just to a boil in a medium heavy saucepan over medium-high heat. Remove the pan from the heat, add the chocolate and salt, and whisk until smooth. Add the Cognac, if using, and whisk until blended. (The fondue can be cooled and refrigerated, covered, for up to 3 days. Gently reheat before serving.)

TRANSFER the fondue to a ceramic fondue pot and keep warm over very low heat. Serve with the dipping ingredients of your choice.

LUSCIOUS CHOCOLATE FONDUE

To serve chocolate fondue properly you must have a way of keeping it warm and in reach of all diners. A ceramic fondue pot is ideal, but do not use a metal pot (save it for cheese), it just gets too hot. My personal favorite is to make the fondue with bittersweet Toblerone and crème fraîche, and to use brioche and pieces of fresh fruit for dipping. The tradition is that if you drop your bread or fruit into the fondue you must kiss the person opposite you. Be sure to provide fondue forks or long bamboo skewers. **SERVES 4 TO 6**

NOTE: **DIPPING POSSIBILITIES** Try sections of oranges, blood oranges, clementines, or tangerines; slices of ripe peaches, pears, nectarines, plums, apricots, bananas, red and green apples, kiwi, or starfruit; cherries or strawberries on the stem; pineapple spears, red and green seedless grapes, or melon balls; chunks of fresh coconut; crystallized ginger or citrus peel; and/or pitted large prunes or dates, plump dried figs, or dried apricots, peaches, or nectarines.

YOU MIGHT ALSO USE MACAROONS; 1-inch squares of pound cake, brownies, or angel food cake; graham crackers, thin crisp wafer cookies, meringues, ladyfingers, gingersnaps, biscotti, shortbread, and/or crispy rice treats; and/or marshmallows or even potato chips and pretzels.

ADDITIONS TO THE FONDUE itself might include peanut or another nut butter, marshmallow cream, unsweetened coconut milk, instant espresso powder, or pure vanilla extract. The liqueurs that I think are particularly good are green Chartreuse, Grand Marnier, amaretto, Chambord, chocolate, coffee, and hazelnut.

4 ounces bittersweet or semisweet chocolate, chopped

5 tablespoons water

3 tablespoons unsalted butter, at room temperature

2 tablespoons confectioners' sugar

¼ teaspoon pure vanilla extract

Eight ½-inch-thick slices brioche or other bread

PREHEAT the oven to 200°F.

MELT the chocolate with the water in a heatproof bowl set over a saucepan of about 1½ inches of nearly simmering water, whisking until smooth. Whisk in 1 tablespoon of the butter, the sugar, and vanilla. Turn off the heat.

HOT CHOCOLATE SAUCE WITH CROUTONS

I got the inspiration for this from *June Platt's Dessert Book*, published in 1942. You can use any bread you choose—some of my friends prefer a fine-crumbed cinnamon raisin, some a chocolate-cherry bread, and others a whole-meal sourdough. Even a dense French-style walnut bread has fans, and most people love brioche. Cut the croutons with a rim of a glass if you don't have a biscuit or cookie cutter. **SERVES 4**

CUT each bread slice into a 3-inch round. Melt 1 tablespoon of the butter in a large nonstick skillet over medium heat. Add 4 of the bread rounds and cook for about 4 minutes, turning once, until browned and crisp. Keep the slices warm in the oven, directly on an oven rack. Wipe out the skillet, melt the remaining 1 tablespoon butter, and cook the remaining bread rounds.

ARRANGE the croutons on 4 dessert plates, and spoon a generous 2 tablespoons of the chocolate sauce over each serving.

SERVE immediately.

½ cup chopped hazelnuts

3 ounces bittersweet
or semisweet chocolate, chopped

½ cup heavy (whipping) cream

3 tablespoons dark brown sugar

Pinch of salt

½ teaspoon pure vanilla extract

4 slices crusty peasant bread
or bread of your choice

2 ripe nectarines or peaches,
pitted and sliced

PREHEAT the oven to 350°F.

TOAST the hazelnuts on a baking sheet for 12 to 15 minutes, until the skins are darkened and the nuts are browned. Pulse the hazelnuts in a food processor, scraping down the sides of the bowl occasionally, for 2 to 3 minutes, until the nuts turn into a paste (or butter). Add the chocolate and pulse until the chocolate is finely ground. Leave the mixture in the processor.

CHOCOLATE-HAZELNUT SPREAD ON TOAST WITH NECTARINES

There is nothing like bread and chocolate, and this is a great version. Thank you to my friend Jean Galton for the recipe; it's adapted from her lovely book Williams-Sonoma's *The Pacific Northwest*. If you use peaches, make sure to peel them; you might also use raspberries, pitted cherries (my favorite), or sliced strawberries. You might decide to whip up a batch of the spread just for adding to your favorite hot chocolate or hot cocoa. Store it in the refrigerator. **SERVES 4**

BRING the cream, sugar, and salt to a boil in a small saucepan over medium heat, stirring to dissolve the sugar. With the motor running, pour the cream mixture through the feed tube and process, scraping down the sides of the bowl occasionally, for 4 to 5 minutes, until the mixture is very smooth. Transfer to a bowl and stir in the vanilla.

TO SERVE, toast the bread slices until golden on both sides. Spread each slice with the chocolate-hazelnut spread, and top with the nectarine slices. Arrange on dessert plates.

PROFITEROLES

½ cup all-purpose flour

2 tablespoons unsweetened cocoa powder

6 tablespoons water

3 tablespoons unsalted butter

1 tablespoon granulated sugar

Pinch of salt

2 large eggs

CHOCOLATE PROFITEROLES
WITH CHOCOLATE ICE CREAM AND CHOCOLATE SAUCE

You can be really creative with this recipe. Fill the profiteroles with your favorite store-bought specialty chocolate ice cream or gelato, or use flavors other than chocolate, or even 3 different flavors for each serving. Dark chocolate, coffee, and hazelnut gelatos would be exquisite. Or try CHOCOLATE SORBET (page 123). And you might instead serve these with CHOCOLATE CARAMEL SAUCE (page 139). SERVES 4

POSITION a rack in the middle of the oven and preheat the oven to 400°F. Butter a large baking sheet.

TO MAKE THE PROFITEROLES: Sift together the flour and cocoa into a small bowl. Bring the water, butter, sugar, and salt to a boil in a medium heavy saucepan over high heat, stirring until the butter is melted. Remove the pan from the heat, add the flour mixture, and stir until the mixture pulls away from the sides of the pan, forming a ball. Transfer the mixture to a large bowl. With an electric mixer on high speed, add the eggs one at a time, beating well after each addition and scraping down the sides of the bowl as necessary. Continue beating until the mixture is smooth, dry looking, and cooled to room temperature.

DROP the mixture by rounded tablespoons onto the baking sheet, forming 12 tall mounds. Smooth each one with dampened fingers. Bake for 20 to 25 minutes, until the pastries are puffed and crisp. Let cool on a wire rack. (The profiteroles can be baked 1 day in advance and stored in an airtight container at room temperature. Reheat on a baking sheet in a preheated 375°F oven for 5 minutes, or until they are crisp, and let them cool on a rack before proceeding.)

¾ cup CHOCOLATE CRÈME FRAÎCHE ICE CREAM (page 119), LUSCIOUS CHOCOLATE CUSTARD ICE CREAM (page 118), BITTERSWEET CHOCOLATE GELATO (page 121), or store-bought chocolate ice cream, slightly softened

Confectioners' sugar for dusting

I cup DEEP DARK CHOCOLATE or MOCHA SAUCE (page 137), warmed

CUT each profiterole crosswise in half with a serrated knife, and discard any uncooked dough in the center. Place about I tablespoon of the ice cream in the bottom of each profiterole, set the tops on the ice cream, and lightly sift confectioners' sugar over each profiterole. Pool about ¼ cup of the chocolate sauce on each of 4 dessert plates and arrange 3 profiteroles on each plate.

SERVE immediately.

2 cups heavy (whipping) cream

3 tablespoons sugar

I teaspoon pure vanilla extract

**One 9-ounce box chocolate
wafer cookies**

BEAT the cream with an electric mixer on medium-high speed in a large bowl until it just forms soft peaks when the beaters are lifted. Add the sugar and vanilla and beat just until the cream forms stiff peaks when the beaters are lifted.

CHOCOLATE WAFER ICEBOX CAKE

This is a dessert I thoroughly enjoyed in childhood and still look forward to today. My recipe is adapted from the one on the package of Nabisco Famous Wafers. You could serve this with just about any fruit or chocolate sauce. Another possibility is to add a fruit or chocolate liqueur to the whipped cream. Try kirschwasser to flavor the cream and serve with **CHERRY SAUCE** (page 140), or raspberry liqueur and **RASPBERRY SAUCE** (page 138). You could also garnish with cocoa nibs or chocolate curls.

SERVES 8

SPREAD a thin layer of cream in the center of an 8-inch square glass baking dish. Spread a thin layer (about ¼ inch) of cream over the top of I cookie. Spread a second cookie with cream and place on top of the first one. Continue until you have a stack of 4 cookies. Carefully lay the stack on its side in the center of the baking dish. Repeat with 20 more cookies, to make 2 side-by-side rolls of 12 cookies each (reserve the remaining cookies). Using a small metal spatula, preferably an offset spatula, generously frost the top and the sides of the rolls with the remaining whipped cream. Refrigerate, loosely covered, for at least 6 hours, or as long as overnight, before serving.

PULSE the remaining cookies in a food processor until finely ground.

TO SERVE, with a sharp knife, cut each roll on a slight diagonal into 4 slices. Lay a slice on each plate and sprinkle with the cookie crumbs.

8 large ripe bananas

½ cup chopped bittersweet chocolate
or semisweet chocolate chips

GRILLED CHOCOLATE-STUFFED BANANAS

One of the highlights of my childhood was summer camp, and one of the best things about camp was these bananas. On special nights, we tossed these into the campfire and they would cook while we sang campfire songs. The timing will depend on how hot your fire is. (If it eases your mind, open one of the packages and check for doneness before removing them all from the fire, but the timing doesn't have to be perfect. However, more done is better than less done.) **SERVES 8**

PREPARE a charcoal fire or heat a gas grill. Without peeling them, make a 5-inch lengthwise slit in each banana, following its natural curve.

PLACE each banana in the center of a 12-inch square of heavy-duty aluminum foil. Fill the slit in each banana with 1 tablespoon of the chocolate chips, pressing them into the banana's flesh, and press the banana closed. Wrap the bananas tightly in the foil and pinch the edges to seal tightly.

COOK the bananas on the grill, preferably covered with a lid, turning occasionally, for 30 to 45 minutes, or until the bananas are very hot and custard-like.

TO SERVE, transfer the still-wrapped bananas to serving plates, and eat with spoons.

4

Nearly everyone agrees that creamy, soft, and spoonable desserts are the most comforting of all. Here I offer several from France, where they really know how to toss together a pudding; one from Austria where they have famous finesse; a couple of silky-smooth creations from Italy; and a few all-American puddings that probably originally came from the English.

puddings + custards + a soufflé

The all-American-style puddings include **MY FAVORITE CHOCOLATE PUDDING** (page 80), a fantastic and fun **CHOCOLATE JELLY** (page 84) that will make the perfect ending to almost any dinner party, and a classic chocolate bread and butter pudding made exotic with dried tart cherries and vivid green pistachios (page 78). From Italy, enjoy the **LUSCIOUS MOCHA TIRAMISÙ** (page 81) or **CHOCOLATE PANNA COTTA** (page 87). The French offerings include a **BITTERSWEET HOT CHOCOLATE SOUFFLÉ** (page 90), dense **VERY CHOCOLATEY POTS DE CRÈME** (page 83), two chocolate mousses (pages 85 and 93), and the out-of-this-world **ULTIMATE CHOCOLATE MARQUISE** (page 88). Although they are significantly different from one another, all are unquestionably in the comfort food, "all is right in the universe" category of desserts.

I cup packed light brown sugar

3 large eggs

4 large egg yolks

4 cups whole milk

4 ounces bittersweet or semisweet chocolate, finely chopped

I cup dried tart cherries, chopped

I½ teaspoons pure vanilla extract

I pound day-old thick-sliced white bread, brioche, or challah, crusts removed

¼ cup (½ stick) unsalted butter, at room temperature

½ cup unsalted toasted shelled natural pistachios, chopped

WHISK together the sugar, eggs, and egg yolks in a large bowl.

BRING the milk just to a boil in a medium saucepan over medium-high heat. Remove the pan from the heat, add the chocolate, and whisk until smooth. Slowly whisk the chocolate mixture, dried cherries, and vanilla into the egg mixture.

SPREAD one side of each slice of bread with butter, then cut them into I-inch squares. Add the bread to the milk mixture and stir gently to moisten all the bread. Let stand at room temperature for 30 minutes.

POSITION a rack in the middle of the oven and preheat the oven to 325°F. Butter a 9-inch square baking pan. Have a large roasting pan ready, and put a kettle of water on to boil for the water bath.

CHOCOLATE, DRIED CHERRY, AND PISTACHIO BREAD AND BUTTER PUDDING

You might use chopped dried peaches and toasted hazelnuts or dried apricots and slivered almonds instead of the cherries and pistachios. Some people like this best served with a pitcher of warm heavy cream.

SERVES 8 TO I0

TRANSFER the bread mixture to the baking pan, spreading the bread evenly in the pan, and top with the pistachios. Place the roasting pan in the oven, place the pan in the roasting pan, and add enough boiling water to the roasting pan to reach halfway up the sides of the baking pan. Bake for I½ hours, or until a knife inserted into the center comes out clean.

REMOVE the pan from the water bath and let cool on a wire rack.

SERVE the bread pudding warm or at room temperature.

½ cup packed dark brown sugar

2 tablespoons granulated sugar

¼ cup unsweetened cocoa powder

2 tablespoons cornstarch

¼ teaspoon salt

2 cups whole milk

4 ounces bittersweet or semisweet chocolate, chopped

1 teaspoon pure vanilla extract

STIR together the brown sugar, granulated sugar, cocoa, cornstarch, and salt with a fork in a large heavy saucepan until the brown sugar is broken up and the mixture is well blended. Add 1 cup of the milk and the chocolate and heat over medium heat, whisking, until the chocolate is melted and the mixture is smooth.

MY FAVORITE CHOCOLATE PUDDING

A perfectly simple recipe for chocolate pudding that's very versatile. Consider adding a tablespoon or so of your favorite liqueur. Or, if you're making this for the lovely Amy Treadwell, assistant editor at Chronicle, add a drop or two of pure mint extract and a simple garnish of crushed hard red-and-white peppermint candies. If you serve it topped with slightly sweetened whipped cream or **CHOCOLATE WHIPPED CREAM** (page 141) and a dusting of finely ground cocoa nibs or crushed **NIB NOUGATINE** (page 129), you'll have three great textures in one dish. **SERVES 4**

WHISK in the remaining 1 cup milk and cook, whisking frequently, for 6 to 8 minutes, until large bubbles pop on the surface and the pudding is thick and smooth. Remove the pan from the heat and whisk in the vanilla, then immediately transfer the pudding to a large bowl or 4 serving bowls or stemmed glasses.

SERVE the pudding hot, warm, at room temperature, or chilled. If not serving immediately, whisk occasionally to keep a skin from forming as it cools.

3 ounces bittersweet
or semisweet chocolate, chopped

1½ cups espresso or
very strong brewed coffee, cooled

3 large eggs, separated

3 tablespoons sugar

I cup mascarpone cheese

I tablespoon Cognac or
other brandy (optional)

¾ cup heavy (whipping) cream

Pinch of salt

About 20 savoiardi (Italian ladyfingers)

Cocoa nibs or CHOCOLATE CURLS
(See page 28) for garnish

MELT the chocolate with ¼ cup of the espresso in a heatproof bowl set over a saucepan of about 1½ inches of nearly simmering water, whisking until smooth. Remove the bowl from the heat and set aside.

BEAT the egg yolks and sugar with an electric mixer on medium-high speed in a medium bowl, occasionally scraping down the sides of the bowl, for 3 to 4 minutes, until thick and pale. Add the mascarpone and Cognac, if using, and beat just until light and fluffy. Add the cream and beat on high speed for about 2 minutes, or until doubled in volume but still soft. Beat in the chocolate mixture.

BEAT the egg whites and salt with clean beaters on medium-high speed in a large bowl just until the whites form soft peaks when the beaters are lifted. With a whisk or a rubber spatula, gently fold the egg whites into the chocolate mixture in 3 batches.

LUSCIOUS MOCHA TIRAMISÙ

If you have a couple of *savoiardi* left over, grind them in a food processor and use them to dust each serving. The topping of cocoa nibs is a perfect textural garnish, even if the Italians didn't think of it. **SERVES 6**

POUR the remaining 1¼ cups espresso into a shallow bowl. Dip 9 or 10 of the *savoiardi*, 2 at a time, into the espresso for about 30 seconds, or just until saturated (if you leave them in too long, they will fall apart) and arrange them in an 8-inch square glass or ceramic dish, cutting or breaking them as necessary to cover the bottom. Cover the *savoiardi* with half of the chocolate mixture. Dip 9 or 10 more *savoiardi* into the remaining espresso, and arrange on top of the chocolate mixture. Spread with the remaining chocolate mixture. Refrigerate, covered, for at least 6 hours, or up to 2 days.

TO SERVE, spoon into goblets, and garnish with the nibs.

1 cup heavy (whipping) cream

4 ounces bittersweet or semisweet chocolate, finely chopped

½ teaspoon pure vanilla extract

3 large egg yolks

¼ cup packed light brown sugar

Pinch of salt

Candied violets, cocoa nibs, slightly sweetened whipped cream, or crème fraîche for garnish (optional)

POSITION a rack in the middle of the oven and preheat the oven to 325°F. Have four 5-ounce ramekins or 6-ounce custard cups and a 9-by-13-inch baking pan ready. Put a kettle of water on to boil for the water bath.

BRING the cream just to a boil in a medium saucepan over medium heat. Remove the pan from the heat, add the chocolate and vanilla, and whisk until smooth.

WHISK together the egg yolks, sugar, and salt in a large bowl, breaking up any large lumps of sugar. Add ½ cup of the cream mixture and whisk gently (to avoid creating air bubbles) to blend well. Pour in the remaining cream mixture in a slow steady stream, whisking constantly. Strain the mixture into a 2-cup glass measure or a bowl with a pour spout.

VERY CHOCOLATEY POTS DE CRÈME

It's easy to see why chocolate pots de crème, simple, elegant, and luscious, is a classic French dish: it's a perfect example of how satisfying just a small amount of a very rich, very good dessert can be. Feel free to infuse the cream with any flavor you choose. You might try lemon or orange zest, Earl Grey tea, or ground toasted hazelnuts; just steep until the flavor is intense enough for you.

SERVES **4**

DIVIDE the custard evenly among the ramekins. Transfer the ramekins to the baking pan, place it in the oven, and add enough boiling water to the pan to reach halfway up the sides of the ramekins. Loosely cover the pan with aluminum foil to keep a skin from forming on the custards.

BAKE for 25 minutes, or until the custards are barely set around the edges and still jiggly in the center. Do not overbake; the custards will set further as they cool.

REMOVE the pan from the oven and, with tongs, a wide spatula, or an oven mitt, carefully transfer the ramekins to a wire rack. Let cool to room temperature, then refrigerate, loosely covered, until thoroughly chilled, at least 3 hours, or up to 1 day.

SERVE the chilled pots de crème in their ramekins, garnished with the violets, if using.

3½ cups water

½ cup packed dark brown sugar

Pinch of salt

8 ounces bittersweet or semisweet chocolate, finely chopped

3 tablespoons plain gelatin

1 teaspoon pure vanilla extract

CHOCOLATE JELLY

I love jellies—real ones. Totally unlike commercial gelatins, they are not too sweet, and they are not rubbery. Since the gelatin company doesn't put the same exact amount of gelatin in each envelope, I call for it by the tablespoon. This is grand served with **CHOCOLATE WHIPPED CREAM** (page 141) and a sprinkling of cocoa nibs or crushed **NIB NOUGATINE** (page 129). You could replace some of the water in the recipe with a tablespoon or two of chocolate or coffee liqueur. **SERVES 4 TO 6**

COAT a 9-inch square baking pan with flavorless oil.

HEAT the water, sugar, and salt in a medium saucepan over medium heat, whisking, until the sugar is dissolved and the water is hot. Remove the pan from the heat, add the chocolate, and whisk until smooth. Pour 1 cup of the mixture into a bowl and sprinkle with the gelatin; set the remaining mixture aside. Let the gelatin stand for about 10 minutes, or until softened.

PLACE the bowl of gelatin in a larger bowl of hot water and stir until the gelatin has dissolved. Whisk the gelatin mixture into the remaining chocolate mixture. Add the vanilla. Pour the mixture through a fine strainer set over a bowl, and let cool to room temperature.

TRANSFER the mixture to the prepared pan and refrigerate, tightly covered, until thoroughly set, at least 3 hours, or up to 1 day.

TO SERVE, cut the jelly into ½-inch cubes with a table knife. Present in glass bowls or stemmed glasses.

I cup heavy (whipping) cream

8 ounces bittersweet or semisweet
chocolate, finely chopped

I teaspoon pure vanilla extract

Pinch of salt

One 8-ounce container crème fraîche or
I cup heavy (whipping) cream

CREAMIEST CHOCOLATE MOUSSE

This is not a classic chocolate mousse, as it doesn't contain eggs, but it is one I think of as a chocolate lover's chocolate mousse. For a great surprise, you can flavor the whipped cream with your favorite liqueur (I love it with Grand Marnier or green Chartreuse), or fold in ¼ to ½ cup **CHOCOLATE-HAZELNUT SPREAD** (page 71), or add a sprinkle of instant espresso or finely chopped candied orange or lemon zest. Garnish the mousse with candied violets or rose petals, fresh unsprayed flower blossoms, or coarse cocoa nibs, or serve it with **CHOCOLATE CHIP MERINGUE COOKIES** (page 103). Please don't cut corners on the quality of the chocolate here— you'll regret it. **SERVES 4**

BRING ½ cup of the heavy cream just to a boil in a medium saucepan over medium heat. Remove the pan from the heat, add the chocolate, and whisk until smooth. Whisk in the vanilla and salt. Transfer to a medium bowl and let cool to room temperature.

WHIP the remaining ½ cup heavy cream and the crème fraîche with an electric mixer on medium-high speed in a medium bowl just until the beaters begin to leave trails in the cream. Add the chocolate in 3 batches and beat on low speed just until well blended; the mixture may look curdled after adding the first batch, but it will smooth out.

TRANSFER to I large glass or porcelain serving bowl or to 4 stemmed glasses. Refrigerate, covered, for at least 30 minutes, and up to 2 days.

1½ cups heavy (whipping) cream

1¼ teaspoons plain gelatin

¼ cup mascarpone cheese or additional heavy (whipping) cream

2 tablespoons sugar

Pinch of salt

2 ounces bittersweet or semisweet chocolate, finely chopped

COAT four 5-ounce ramekins or 6-ounce custard cups lightly with flavorless oil.

POUR ¼ cup of the cream into a small heatproof bowl, sprinkle the gelatin over it, and let stand for about 10 minutes, or until softened. Place the bowl in a larger bowl of hot water and stir until the gelatin has dissolved.

CHOCOLATE PANNA COTTA

Panna cotta has become a very popular dessert on our shores these last few years, and for good reason. It's a luscious, totally Italian custard, no eggs, just cream and flavorings. This is good served alone or with the slightest dusting of **NIB NOUGATINE** (page 129), finely ground cocoa nibs, or shaved chocolate. Panna cotta is usually vanilla—this one is for chocolate lovers. **SERVES 4**

MEANWHILE, bring the remaining 1¼ cups cream, the mascarpone, sugar, and salt just to a boil in a medium saucepan over medium heat. Remove the pan from the heat, add the chocolate, and whisk until smooth.

ADD the gelatin mixture to the chocolate mixture and stir until well blended. Pour through a fine strainer into a 4-cup glass measure or a bowl with a pour spout. Divide the mixture evenly among the ramekins, and let cool to room temperature.

REFRIGERATE the panna cotta, loosely covered, until set and thoroughly chilled, at least 3 hours, or up to 1 day.

TO SERVE, dip the ramekins one at a time into a bowl of hot water for about 5 seconds, then run a table knife around the edges of the custard and invert onto a chilled serving plate.

I pound bittersweet or semisweet chocolate, chopped

I cup (2 sticks) unsalted butter, at room temperature

¼ cup sugar

I tablespoon Cognac or other brandy or liqueur (optional)

6 large eggs, separated

2 large egg yolks

Pinch of salt

BUTTER an 8-by-4-inch loaf pan and line with 2 sheets of plastic wrap, one going the long way and one going the short way, leaving an overhang of several inches on all sides.

MELT the chocolate and butter in a large heatproof bowl set over a saucepan of about 1½ inches of nearly simmering water, whisking until smooth. Whisk in the sugar and Cognac, if using, until well blended.

REMOVE the bowl from the heat and with an electric mixer on low speed, beat in the egg yolks one at a time, beating well after each addition and occasionally scraping down the sides of the bowl.

ULTIMATE CHOCOLATE MARQUISE

This may be my favorite dessert. It keeps so well you can freeze it for up to a month, then when someone drops by, you can instantly pull it out of the freezer and offer a slice. Also—it's so easy to make but looks difficult and "restauranty." It's wonderful with softly whipped cream, but you can doll it up with a drizzle of **CHOCOLATE SYRUP** (page 140), or a spoonful of **CHERRY** (page 140), **BLACKBERRY, STRAWBERRY,** or **RASPBERRY SAUCE** (page 138). It can be refrigerated rather than frozen, but it's more difficult to cut and doesn't last as long.

SERVES 10 OR MORE

BEAT the egg whites and salt with clean beaters on medium-high speed in a large deep bowl just until the whites form stiff peaks when the beaters are lifted. With a whisk or a rubber spatula, fold one-third of the egg whites into the chocolate mixture. Fold in the remaining egg whites in 2 batches just until well blended.

TRANSFER the mixture to the prepared pan, pushing it into the corners and smoothing the top with a rubber spatula. Cover with the overhanging plastic wrap and then wrap tightly with aluminum foil. Freeze for at least 6 hours.

TO SERVE, unwrap the pan, fold back the plastic wrap, and run a table knife around the edges of the pan to loosen the marquise. Place a serving platter over the pan, invert the pan onto it, and release the marquise by pulling on the edges of the plastic wrap. Remove the plastic wrap and smooth the edges of the marquise with a small warm metal spatula if necessary. Cut into ½-inch-thick slices with a sharp knife dipped in very warm water and wiped dry between each slice, and place on chilled dessert plates. (You can tightly rewrap and freeze any leftover marquise.)

7 ounces bittersweet or
semisweet chocolate, chopped

5 large eggs, separated

¼ cup (½ stick) unsalted butter,
at room temperature

5 large egg whites

Pinch of salt

¼ cup sugar

Slightly sweetened whipped cream or
crème fraîche for serving (optional)

POSITION a rack in the middle of the oven and preheat the oven to 425°F. Butter a 1½-quart soufflé dish and dust it with sugar, shaking out any excess. Have a 9-by-13-inch baking pan ready, and put a kettle of water on to boil for the water bath.

MELT the chocolate in a heatproof bowl set over a saucepan of about 1½ inches of nearly simmering water, whisking until smooth. Remove the bowl from the heat and whisk in the egg yolks and butter until well blended.

BITTERSWEET HOT CHOCOLATE SOUFFLÉ

Although the classic soufflé base calls for flour, for chocolate soufflé, I prefer it made without—I think the chocolate flavor comes through better. One of my favorite things to do with a soufflé, especially this one, is to hollow out the top with a spoon and fill in the hole with softly whipped cream or crème fraîche just before serving. You could even use CHOCOLATE WHIPPED CREAM (page 141). SERVES 4 TO 6

BEAT the egg whites and salt with an electric mixer on medium-high speed in a large bowl until the whites form soft peaks when the beaters are lifted. Beat in the sugar about 1 tablespoon at a time, beating well after each addition, and beat just until the whites form stiff peaks when the beaters are lifted.

WITH a wisk or a rubber spatula, fold one-quarter of the whites into the chocolate mixture to lighten it. Fold in the remaining whites gently but thoroughly, and pour the mixture into the soufflé dish. Place the dish in the baking pan, place it in the oven, and add enough boiling water to the pan to reach halfway up the sides of the soufflé dish. Bake for 40 minutes, or until the soufflé is set but the center is still jiggly and soft.

SERVE immediately, with the whipped cream, if using.

4 ounces bittersweet or semisweet chocolate, chopped

¼ cup heavy (whipping) cream

¼ cup sugar

4 large eggs, separated

Pinch of salt

BLACK VELVET CHOCOLATE MOUSSE

Luscious and foamy, this is a classic chocolate mousse, and one you will make again and again. I promise. **SERVES 4**

MELT the chocolate with the cream in a heatproof bowl set over a saucepan of about 1½ inches of nearly simmering water, whisking until smooth. Add the sugar in 2 batches and whisk until well blended. Remove the bowl from the heat and whisk in the egg yolks one at a time, whisking well after each addition.

BEAT the egg whites and salt with an electric mixer on medium-high speed in a large deep bowl just until the whites form stiff peaks when the beaters are lifted. With a whisk or a rubber spatula, fold one-third of the chocolate mixture into the egg whites. Fold in the remaining chocolate mixture in 2 batches just until well blended.

TRANSFER to a serving bowl or to 4 stemmed glasses. Refrigerate, covered, for at least 4 hours, or up to 2 days before serving.

Whatever would we do without cookies? I'd rather not even think about it. It's impossible, and silly even to try, to improve on the original Toll House cookie, but here you'll find several other chippers you might like just as much. First give the **CHOCO-LATE-CHOCOLATE CHUNK COOKIES** (page 97) a try. They are a very sophisticated version, with more chocolate than in your typical Toll House, and the same buttery rich flavor. Most chocolate chip cookies are chewy, but I offer another style in the **CRISP CHOCOLATE CHIP COOKIES WITH DRIED CHERRIES AND PISTA-CHIOS** (page 98).

cookies

They are thinner and crisper, and have the out-of-the-ordinary additions of dried cherries and pistachios. **CHOCOLATE CHIP MERINGUE COOKIES** (page 103) are worlds apart from classic chocolate chip cookies, but, boy, are they good. They are simple, a great flavor and texture combination, and far better than the sum of their parts. You'll find the way the meringue and the chocolate melt differently in your mouth tantalizing. And **FRENCH CHOCOLATE MACAROONS** (page 100), both wonderfully crisp and creamy, are one of the best things about French cuisine. One of my favorite combinations is chocolate and caramel. You'll find that blend in the **TURTLE BAR COOKIES** (page 112), where it works especially well, and in the **GANACHE-FILLED BROWN SUGAR BARS** (page 111), which you will adore. Trust me.

What could be better than a deeply flavored chocolate cookie that is chewy on the inside and crisp on the outside? The **CHOCOLATIEST CRINKLES** (page 105) have that great high-contrast appearance and texture we all love in crinkle or crackle cookies. **BUTTERY CHOCOLATE WAFERS** (page 106) are also really easy to make and a terrific cookie to count on. You can freeze the rolls of dough and bake them fresh when a friend drops by, or for any unexpected occasion, or you can freeze the baked cookies (they defrost quickly). They are very chocolatey and very pleasing. Any collection of cookie recipes must include shortbread, and the **MOCHA SHORTBREAD** (page 107) here has a great texture and lots of chocolate flavor, enhanced by the coffee. Very adult, these are not kid stuff. And, finally, you'll find two of that all-American classic sweet, brownies, here. I've always been fond of Katharine Hepburn and her brownies. They are a great old-fashioned, uncomplicated version, and remind me of simpler times. The **NIB NOUGATINE BROWNIES** (page 110) are a more updated, stylish version, but one that still has the great fudgy texture I think all brownies should have.

11 ounces bittersweet or
semisweet chocolate, chopped

3 tablespoons unsalted butter

1 teaspoon instant
espresso powder (optional)

½ cup packed dark brown sugar

2 large eggs

1 teaspoon pure vanilla extract

⅓ cup all-purpose flour

¼ teaspoon baking powder

Pinch of salt

1 cup chopped toasted hazelnuts
and/or pecans

¼ cup cocoa nibs (optional)

POSITION a rack in the middle of the oven and preheat the oven to 350°F. Butter 2 baking sheets.

MELT 8 ounces of the chocolate with the butter and espresso powder, if using, in a heatproof bowl set over a saucepan of about 1½ inches of nearly simmering water, whisking until smooth. Remove the bowl from the heat.

CHOCOLATE–CHOCOLATE CHUNK COOKIES

In the early 1980s, I worked for David of David's Cookies in the kitchen of his restaurant, Manhattan Market, and I ate millions of his cookies. I still miss them. I loved the big chunks of chocolate he used and that he used so many of them. When I gave a batch of these cookies to my super upstairs neighbors, Jim Rescigna and Jack Raftery, Jim said, "Lord, if this is heaven, take me now." My sentiments exactly. **MAKES 15 COOKIES**

BEAT the sugar, eggs, and vanilla with an electric mixer on medium speed in a large bowl until smooth and well blended. Whisk in the chocolate mixture. Sift the flour, baking powder, and salt over the mixture and whisk until well blended. Stir in the remaining 3 ounces chopped chocolate, the nuts, and cocoa nibs, if using.

DROP the batter, using a scant ¼ cup for each cookie, about 2 inches apart on the prepared baking sheets, placing 8 cookies on the first sheet and 7 on the second. Bake, one sheet at a time, for 10 to 12 minutes, or until the tops are slightly cracked and the surface has a dull sheen.

COOL the cookies on the baking sheets on wire racks for 10 minutes, then transfer to the racks to cool completely. (The cookies can be stored in an airtight container at room temperature for up to 3 days.)

1¾ cups all-purpose flour

¾ teaspoon salt

¾ teaspoon baking soda

¾ cup (1½ sticks) unsalted butter, at room temperature

½ cup packed light brown sugar

¼ cup granulated sugar

3 tablespoons light corn syrup

2 tablespoons whole milk

2 teaspoons pure vanilla extract

1 cup miniature bittersweet or semisweet chocolate chips

¾ cup unsalted toasted shelled natural pistachios, chopped

¾ cup dried tart cherries, chopped

POSITION the oven racks in the upper and lower thirds of the oven and preheat the oven to 375°F. Butter 2 baking sheets.

WHISK together the flour, salt, and baking soda in a small bowl.

BEAT the butter with an electric mixer on medium-high speed in a large bowl until light and fluffy. Add the brown and granulated sugars and beat until light and fluffy. Beat in the corn syrup until well blended. Beat in the milk and vanilla. Reduce the speed to low, add the flour mixture, and beat just until smooth, scraping down the sides of the bowl with a rubber spatula as necessary. With a rubber spatula, stir in the chocolate chips, pistachios, and cherries. Press the dough together with your hands.

CRISP CHOCOLATE CHIP COOKIES WITH DRIED CHERRIES AND PISTACHIOS

Although they're flatter and crisper than the classic Toll House cookie, these still have lots of chocolate chips. "Natural" pistachios are the green ones, not the ones that have been dyed red.

MAKES A GENEROUS 4 DOZEN COOKIES

SHAPE the dough into 1-inch balls and place them about 2 inches apart on the prepared baking sheets. With the palm of your hand or the flat bottom of a glass, flatten each ball to a disk about ⅜ inch thick. Bake for 4 minutes, switch the position of the pans, and bake for 4 to 6 minutes longer, until the cookies are light golden brown.

COOL the cookies on the baking sheets on wire racks for 3 minutes, then transfer to the racks to cool completely. The cookies will crisp as they cool. (The cookies can be stored in an airtight container at room temperature for up to 3 days.)

MACAROONS

½ cup blanched whole almonds

1¾ cups confectioners' sugar

3 tablespoons unsweetened
cocoa powder

3 large egg whites

Pinch of salt

2 teaspoons granulated sugar

continued

POSITION a rack in the middle of the oven and preheat the oven to 400°F. Line 2 large baking sheets with parchment paper.

TO MAKE THE MACAROONS: Pulse the almonds with 1 cup of the confectioners' sugar in a food processor until finely ground. Add the cocoa powder and the remaining ¾ cup confectioners' sugar and pulse until well blended.

BEAT the egg whites with the salt with an electric mixer on medium-high speed in a large bowl just until the whites form soft peaks when the beaters are lifted. Add the granulated sugar and beat just until the whites form stiff peaks when the beaters are lifted. With a whisk or a rubber spatula, gently fold in the almond mixture.

FRENCH CHOCOLATE MACAROONS

First made by convent nuns during the eighteenth century, these are not at all like the macaroons most of us grew up with. They are one of my most favorite things about being in Paris, and I love walking through the city nibbling on them. I usually get them from either Dalloyau or Laduree.

If you're not going to Paris soon, whip these up and make believe. You'll love the textural contrast between the crisp cookies and the luscious creamy ganache filling.

MAKES ABOUT 4 DOZEN COOKIES

TRANSFER the batter to a pastry bag fitted with a ½-inch plain tip. Pipe out 1-inch-diameter mounds about 2 inches apart on the prepared baking sheets. Bake, one sheet at a time, for 6 to 8 minutes, until the tops are cracked and appear dry but the macaroons are still slightly soft to the touch.

TRANSFER the cookies, still on the parchment paper, to barely dampened kitchen towels and let cool for 5 minutes. Carefully peel the paper off the macaroons and transfer to wire racks to cool completely. (The macaroons can be made 1 day in advance and stored in layers separated by wax paper in an airtight container.)

continued

FILLING

½ cup heavy (whipping) cream

2 tablespoons unsweetened cocoa powder

5 ounces bittersweet or semisweet chocolate, finely chopped

½ cup (1 stick) unsalted butter, at room temperature

FRENCH CHOCOLATE MACAROONS *continued*

TO MAKE THE FILLING: Bring the cream just to a boil in a medium saucepan over high heat. Remove the pan from the heat and whisk in the cocoa powder. Add the chocolate and butter and whisk until smooth. Let cool to room temperature, then refrigerate, covered, for at least 30 minutes, or until the filling is firm enough to hold its shape when spread.

IF DESIRED, transfer the filling to a pastry bag fitted with a ½-inch plain tip. Pipe the filling, or spread it with a table knife, generously on the flat side of half of the macaroons. Top with the remaining macaroons, flat-side down, pressing together gently to form sandwiches. (The cookies can be stored in layers separated by wax paper in an airtight container in the refrigerator for up to 2 days.)

3 large egg whites,
at room temperature

¼ teaspoon cream of tartar

Pinch of salt

½ cup sugar

I teaspoon pure vanilla extract

¾ cup miniature bittersweet
or semisweet chocolate chips

¼ cup cocoa nibs (optional)

POSITION the oven racks in the upper and lower thirds of the oven and preheat the oven to 275°F. Line 2 large baking sheets with parchment or wax paper.

CHOCOLATE CHIP MERINGUE COOKIES

These cookies have a lot going for them—that great meringue texture, crunchy on the outside and a little bit chewy and gooey in the middle, and lots of chocolate chips. If you'd like to gild the lily, dip part of the cookies in melted chocolate before serving, or give them a light coating of cocoa. You might also make the cookies a little smaller and sandwich them with the ganache from the **FRENCH CHOCOLATE MACAROONS** (page 100). I know it's unconventional, but I like the meringues to get a little brown— they taste better.

MAKES ABOUT 3 DOZEN COOKIES

BEAT the egg whites, cream of tartar, and salt with an electric mixer on medium-high speed in a large bowl just until the whites form soft peaks when the beaters are lifted. Add the sugar about I tablespoon at a time, and beat just until the whites form stiff peaks when the beaters are lifted. Beat in the vanilla. With a whisk or a rubber spatula, gently fold in the chocolate chips and nibs, if using.

DROP the batter by heaping tablespoons about 1½ inches apart on the prepared baking sheets. Bake, switching the position of the pans after 30 minutes, for I hour, or until the meringues are light golden brown and dry on the outside but still a little soft on the inside.

COOL on the baking sheets on wire racks for 10 minutes, then carefully peel the meringues off the parchment paper and transfer to the racks to cool completely. (The cookies can be stored in layers separated by wax paper in an airtight container at room temperature for several days.)

5 ounces bittersweet or
semisweet chocolate, chopped

¾ cup plus 2 tablespoons
all-purpose flour

½ teaspoon baking soda

¼ teaspoon salt

½ cup (1 stick) unsalted butter,
at room temperature

½ cup granulated sugar

½ cup packed dark brown sugar

1 large egg

1½ teaspoons pure vanilla extract

½ cup confectioners' sugar

MELT the chocolate in a heatproof bowl set over a saucepan of about 1½ inches of nearly simmering water, whisking until smooth. Remove the bowl from the heat and set aside.

WHISK together the flour, baking soda, and salt in a small bowl. Beat the butter with an electric mixer on medium speed in a large bowl until light and fluffy. Add the granulated and brown sugars and beat until smooth. Add the melted chocolate and beat until well blended. Add the egg and vanilla and beat until well blended. Reduce the speed to low and add the flour mixture in 3 batches, beating just until well blended after each addition. Transfer the dough to a small bowl, cover, and refrigerate until firm, at least 2 hours, or as long as overnight.

CHOCOLATIEST CRINKLES

Call these what you like, crinkles, cracks, or crackles—whatever you call them, they are chewy on the inside and crisp on the outside, one of my favorite textures for cookies. When I want a chocolate cookie, this is usually the first one I think of. Serve these with espresso and Sambuca, afternoon tea, or ice cold milk. They're also great with ice cream, and nobody would trade them away if they were in her lunchbox.

MAKES ABOUT 4 DOZEN COOKIES

POSITION the oven racks in the upper and lower thirds of the oven and preheat the oven to 375°F. Butter 2 large baking sheets.

PLACE the confectioners' sugar in a small bowl. Shape the dough into 1-inch balls, roll in the confectioners' sugar to coat thoroughly and heavily, and place 2 inches apart on the prepared baking sheets. Bake for 8 minutes, or until the tops spring back when lightly touched.

COOL the cookies on the baking sheets on wire racks for 2 minutes, then transfer to the racks to cool completely. (The cookies can be stored in layers separated by wax paper in an airtight container at room temperature for several days.)

6 ounces bittersweet or semisweet chocolate, chopped

6 tablespoons (¾ stick) unsalted butter, at room temperature

¼ cup packed light brown sugar

I teaspoon pure vanilla extract

I cup all-purpose flour

¼ teaspoon salt

MELT the chocolate in a heatproof bowl set over a saucepan of about I½ inches of nearly simmering water, whisking until smooth. Remove the bowl from the heat and set aside.

BEAT the butter with an electric mixer on medium-high speed in a medium bowl until light and fluffy. Add the sugar and beat until light and fluffy. Add the melted chocolate and the vanilla and beat until smooth. Reduce the speed to low and beat in the flour and salt just until blended.

BUTTERY CHOCOLATE WAFERS

Sometimes slice-and-bake cookies are just the ticket. This recipe is easily doubled, so you can keep some of the dough or baked cookies on hand in the freezer ready for unexpected guests. The cookies may break when you slice the dough, but if they do, simply put them back together on the baking sheet; they'll look fine when baked. I recommend using a serrated slicing knife and direct pressure, rather than a sawing motion, for cutting them, which is much less likely to crack the dough.

Because the recipe is so simple, with so few ingredients, it's important to use the freshest butter and a really high-quality chocolate.

MAKES ABOUT 2 DOZEN COOKIES

DIVIDE the dough in half. Place each piece on a sheet of wax paper and shape each one into a rectangular log about 4 inches long and I inch high, with 4 squared-off sides. Wrap the logs tightly in the wax paper and refrigerate until firm, at least 6 hours, or as long as overnight.

POSITION a rack in the middle of the oven and preheat the oven to 350°F. Line 2 large baking sheets with parchment or wax paper.

LET the logs stand at room temperature for 20 minutes before slicing. With a sharp knife, preferably a serrated one, cut each log into ⅜-inch-thick slices, using one firm downward stroke rather than a sawing motion, and place the slices about I inch apart on the prepared baking sheets. Bake, one sheet at a time, for 8 to IO minutes, until the tops spring back when touched lightly.

COOL the cookies completely on the baking sheets on wire racks. (The cookies can be stored in an airtight container at room temperature for 3 to 4 days.)

2 cups all-purpose flour

½ cup unsweetened cocoa powder

2 teaspoons instant espresso powder

¼ teaspoon salt

I cup (2 sticks) unsalted butter, at room temperature

¾ cup plus 2 tablespoons confectioners' sugar

I teaspoon pure vanilla extract

MOCHA SHORTBREAD

These are very delicate and "sandy," which is a good thing for shortbread. You can make two crossed skewer imprints on each cookie, and they will look like the tops of screws; or make them look like little buttons by punching out four holes with the end of a skewer. These make the ultimate sandwich cookies, with about a teaspoon of the ganache mixture from the FRENCH CHOCOLATE MACAROONS (page 100) between each pair of cookies. These are great with coffee, iced or hot, or a chocolate drink, iced or hot. The most important thing here is to roll the dough evenly, so the cookies will bake evenly.

MAKES ABOUT 5 DOZEN COOKIES

WHISK together the flour, cocoa, espresso powder, and salt in a medium bowl.

BEAT the butter with an electric mixer on medium-high speed in a large deep bowl until light and fluffy. Add the sugar and beat until light and fluffy. Scrape down the sides of the bowl with a rubber spatula, and beat in the vanilla until well blended. Reduce the speed to low and add the flour mixture in 3 batches, scraping down the sides of the bowl after each addition and beating just until well blended. The dough will be crumbly; knead it in the bowl until it comes together.

DIVIDE the dough into 4 equal pieces. Shape each piece into a 4-inch disk and wrap each in wax paper. Refrigerate until firm enough to roll, at least 45 minutes, or as long as overnight.

POSITION a rack in the middle of the oven and preheat the oven to 325°F. Have 2 large baking sheets ready.

WORK with one portion of dough at a time, keeping the remainder refrigerated. If the dough has been refrigerated overnight, let each disk sit out for 15 minutes or so before rolling. Place each disk between 2 sheets of wax paper, and roll out the dough ¼ inch thick. Cut out rounds with a 2-inch scallop-edged biscuit cutter or other 2-inch cutter and transfer to the baking sheets, spacing them about I inch apart. Gather the scraps and roll them out to make more cookies. Prick each cookie 2 or 3 times with a fork.

BAKE, one sheet at a time, for 6 to 8 minutes, until the cookies are slightly puffed and the tops spring back when touched lightly.

COOL the cookies on the baking sheets on wire racks for 3 minutes, then carefully transfer the cookies to the racks to cool completely. (The cookies can be stored in an airtight container at room temperature for up to 3 days.)

- ½ cup (1 stick) unsalted butter
- 2 ounces unsweetened chocolate, chopped
- 1 cup sugar
- 2 large eggs, lightly beaten
- ½ teaspoon pure vanilla extract
- ¼ cup all-purpose flour
- ¼ teaspoon salt
- 1 cup walnuts, chopped

I got this recipe close to twenty years ago from *Family Circle* magazine, and these great old-fashioned brownies, almost like candy, have long been my benchmark. I've always thought Katharine Hepburn a kindred spirit because she described herself as someone who ate chocolate every day—and I like that in a person! Serve the brownies as is or dress them up with a dab of crème fraîche and chocolate curls added to each one just before serving. Just make sure to let the brownies cool completely before you do any cutting, and use a sharp knife rinsed in hot water and dried between each cut. They're easiest to cut if you chill them before cutting, but they are best served at room temperature. If you'd like to freeze them, wrap each one individually. **MAKES 9 LARGE BROWNIES**

KATHARINE HEPBURN'S BROWNIES

POSITION a rack in the middle of the oven and preheat the oven to 325°F. Butter and flour an 8-inch square baking pan.

MELT the butter and chocolate in a heatproof bowl set over a saucepan of about 1½ inches of nearly simmering water, whisking until smooth. Remove the bowl from the heat, add the sugar, eggs, and vanilla, and whisk until well blended. Whisk in the flour and salt just until well blended. Stir in the walnuts. Transfer the batter to the prepared pan.

BAKE for 40 minutes, or until a wooden pick inserted in the center comes out sticky, with just a few crumbs clinging to it, but is not wet; do not overbake.

COOL completely in the pan on a wire rack. Chill if you have the time, then cut into 9 brownies.

1 cup (2 sticks) unsalted butter

4 ounces unsweetened
chocolate, chopped

1¾ cups sugar

4 large eggs

1½ teaspoons pure vanilla extract

¼ teaspoon salt

½ cup all-purpose flour

¼ cup unsweetened cocoa powder

½ cup crushed NIB NOUGATINE
(page 129)

POSITION a rack in the middle of the oven and preheat the oven to 350°F. Butter a 9-by-12-inch baking pan. Line the bottom with a piece of aluminum foil large enough to overhang the long sides by at least 1 inch, and butter the foil.

MELT the butter with the chocolate in a heatproof bowl set over a saucepan of about 1½ inches of nearly simmering water, whisking until smooth. Remove the bowl from the heat and set aside.

NIB NOUGATINE BROWNIES

Brownies can be flavored in countless ways, and this is one of my favorites. To me, the most important aspect of a brownie is texture: I like fudgy brownies, dense bars with a moist, intensely chocolate interior. I have no use for cakey brownies—I'd rather have cake. (Speaking of cakes, brownies make a fabulous birthday "cake"; piled high on a cake stand, they look festive and are a true crowd-pleaser.) The crushed nougatine should be in about quarter-inch pieces. MAKES 24 BROWNIES

BEAT the sugar and eggs in a medium bowl with an electric mixer on medium-high speed for 3 minutes, or until thick and pale. Beat in the vanilla and salt. With a whisk or a rubber spatula, gently fold in the chocolate mixture just until blended. Sift the flour and cocoa over the chocolate mixture and fold in just until blended. Fold in ¼ cup of the nib nougatine.

TRANSFER the batter to the prepared pan, spreading it evenly with a rubber spatula. Top with the remaining ¼ cup nougatine. Bake for 30 to 35 minutes, until a wooden pick inserted in the center comes out sticky with just a few crumbs clinging to it, but is not wet; do not overbake. Let cool completely in the pan on a wire rack.

LIFT up the edges of the foil, and transfer the brownies to a cutting board. Discard the foil. Cut the brownies lengthwise into 4 strips, then cut each strip crosswise into 6 bars.

1¾ cups all-purpose flour

¼ teaspoon salt

1 cup (2 sticks) unsalted butter, at room temperature

1¾ cups packed dark brown sugar

2 large eggs, at room temperature

1½ teaspoons pure vanilla extract

½ cup heavy (whipping) cream

8 ounces bittersweet or semisweet chocolate, chopped

POSITION a rack in the middle of the oven and preheat the oven to 350°F. Lightly butter the bottom of a 10-by-15-inch baking sheet. Line the pan with wax paper, then butter and flour the paper and the sides of the pan.

WHISK together the flour and salt in a small bowl. Beat the butter and sugar with an electric mixer on medium speed in a large bowl for about 3 minutes, until light and fluffy. Beat in the eggs one at a time, beating well after each addition. Beat in the vanilla. Reduce the speed to low and add the flour mixture in 3 batches, beating just until well blended. The batter will be fairly stiff.

GANACHE-FILLED BROWN SUGAR BARS

Another great recipe from Judith Sutton, who is very knowledgeable about how to put chocolate, butter, and cream to their best use! One meaning of the French word *ganache* is "bungler," and the folklore is that in the nineteenth century, an apprentice in a Paris pastry shop who spilled hot cream into a bowl of chopped chocolate was called *ganache* by his boss. But the chef stirred the chocolate and cream together to see if it could be salvaged, and the rest is history. Another bit of trivia—the word also translates as a "well-padded easy chair." I like that, don't you? **MAKES 32 BARS**

SPREAD the batter evenly in the pan with a long metal spatula. Bake for 18 to 20 minutes, until a wooden pick inserted in the center comes out clean but not dry; do not overbake. Transfer the pan to a wire rack to cool completely.

BRING the cream just to a boil in a small saucepan over medium heat. Meanwhile, process the chocolate in a food processor until finely ground. With the motor running, slowly add the cream to the chocolate and process until smooth. Transfer the ganache to a medium bowl and let stand at room temperature for at least 30 minutes to set; it should be spreadable but not runny.

COVER the baking pan with a large wire rack and invert the pan. Remove the pan and peel off the wax paper. Invert the cake again onto a large cutting board. Cut the cake crosswise in half with a long serrated knife. Spread the ganache evenly on one half of the cake to within ⅛ inch of the edges. Carefully set the other cake half on top, matching the cut edges. Cover and refrigerate until the ganache is set, at least 2 hours or up to 2 days.

TO SERVE, trim the uncut edges of the cake with a long serrated knife. Cut the cake lengthwise into 4 strips, then cut each strip crosswise into 8 rectangles. Serve chilled or at room temperature.

CRUST

1 cup all-purpose flour

¼ cup granulated sugar

Pinch of salt

6 tablespoons (¾ stick) cold unsalted butter, cut into small pieces

2 to 3 tablespoons ice cold water

POSITION a rack in the middle of the oven and preheat the oven to 425°F. Butter a 9-inch square baking pan, line it with a piece of aluminum foil large enough to overhang two opposite sides by at least 2 inches, and butter the foil.

TURTLE BAR COOKIES

I also like these, very much, with almonds or cashews instead of pecans. It's important to spread the pastry evenly in the pan so it bakes evenly. The caramel topping takes quite a while to cool because all that sugar holds the heat for a long time, so figure on at least an hour. You'll be happiest if you cut these into small cookies—they are rich. **MAKES 2 DOZEN BARS**

TO MAKE THE CRUST: Whisk together the flour, sugar, and salt in a medium bowl. Cut in the butter with a pastry blender or 2 knives used scissors-fashion until the butter is the size of small peas. Sprinkle 1 tablespoon of the water over the flour mixture, stirring gently with a fork to distribute the moisture evenly. Continue adding water until the dough just begins to come together when a small bit is pressed between your fingers; do not overwork the dough.

PRESS the dough evenly into the bottom of the prepared pan. Prick all over with a fork. Bake for 15 to 20 minutes, until light golden brown.

COOL completely in the pan on a wire rack.

1¼ cups packed light brown sugar

½ cup heavy (whipping) cream

⅓ cup light corn syrup

3 tablespoons unsalted butter

1½ teaspoons apple cider vinegar

¼ teaspoon salt

1 teaspoon pure vanilla extract

¾ cup toasted pecans, coarsely chopped

¼ cup cocoa nibs

4 ounces bittersweet or semisweet chocolate, chopped

TO MAKE THE TOPPING: Stir together the sugar, cream, corn syrup, butter, vinegar, and salt in a large heavy saucepan, breaking up any large lumps of sugar. Bring to a boil over medium-high heat, stirring until the sugar is dissolved. Reduce the heat to medium, and boil, stirring frequently, for 5 minutes, or until the mixture is dark golden brown and thickened. Remove the pan from the heat, carefully stir in the vanilla, and continue to stir until the bubbling stops. Pour the hot filling over the crust. Sprinkle evenly with the pecans and nibs. Cool completely on a wire rack, at least 1 hour.

MELT the chocolate in a heatproof bowl set over a saucepan of about 1½ inches of nearly simmering water, whisking until smooth. With a fork, drizzle the chocolate over the bars. Let cool to room temperature, then refrigerate for at least 30 minutes, or until the chocolate and caramel are set.

LIFT up the ends of the foil, and transfer the cookies to a cutting board. Discard the foil. Cut the cookies into 4 strips in one direction, then cut each strip into 6 bars.

There's nothing like an ice cream dessert to make everyone's eyes light up. It doesn't have to be fancy, it doesn't have to take a long time to make, but if it's chocolate and if it's ice cream, who wouldn't be happy to have it set in front of them? Making your own ice cream is a breeze; you just need a little time to let it chill—and if you're impatient, like me, you can use a **"QUICK-CHILL METHOD"** (see page 123) so the mix doesn't have to spend several hours in the refrigerator before you freeze it.

frozen chocolate desserts

There are lots of good inexpensive ice cream makers out there these days. If you don't already have one, pick one up and you can have homemade frozen desserts in a flash. Start with **LUSCIOUS CHOCOLATE CUSTARD ICE CREAM** (page 118), **CHOCOLATE CRÈME FRAÎCHE ICE CREAM** (page 119), **BITTERSWEET CHOCOLATE GELATO** (page 121), or **CHOCOLATE SORBET** (page 123). When you make these frozen chocolate desserts, you'll discover they have delightfully different textures, and it will take serious concentration to decide which is your favorite. You can use either homemade or store-bought ice cream for **NIB NOUGATINE CHOCOLATE ICE CREAM SUNDAES** (page 116) and the **BROWNIE HOT FUDGE ICE CREAM SUNDAES** (page 122). Combining these ice creams and other frozen treats with the toppings in the sauce chapter will give you tons of combinations and permutations and an endless supply of fun desserts.

¾ cup DEEP DARK CHOCOLATE
or MOCHA SAUCE (page 137)
or other chocolate sauce, warmed

LUSCIOUS CHOCOLATE CUSTARD ICE
CREAM (page 118) or 2 pints store-
bought chocolate ice cream or gelato

CHOCOLATE WHIPPED CREAM (page 141)

¼ cup crushed or finely ground
NIB NOUGATINE (page 129)

4 ripe strawberries
on the stem (optional)

NIB NOUGATINE CHOCOLATE
ICE CREAM SUNDAES

This is totally chocolate, but you could use any flavor ice cream you choose: chocolate peanut butter, Chunky Monkey, mint, peach, or even ginger. The Nib Nougatine should be in quarter-inch pieces or less, or finely ground. Use store-bought chocolate sauce if you prefer. **SERVES 4**

SPOON 1 tablespoon of the chocolate sauce into the bottom of each of 4 sundae dishes. Add 1 scoop of the ice cream to each, then top with another tablespoon of the chocolate sauce. Repeat with 1 more scoop of ice cream and 1 tablespoon of the sauce in each dish. Add a generous dollop of the whipped cream to each sundae, garnish with the nib nougatine and strawberries, if using, and serve immediately.

8 ounces bittersweet or
semisweet chocolate, chopped

9 large egg yolks

1 cup packed light brown sugar

1½ cups whole milk

1½ cups heavy (whipping) cream

Pinch of salt

1 teaspoon pure vanilla extract

MELT the chocolate in a heatproof bowl set over a saucepan of about 1½ inches of nearly simmering water, whisking until smooth. Remove the bowl from the heat and let cool.

MEANWHILE, beat the egg yolks and sugar with an electric mixer on medium-high speed in a large deep bowl, scraping down the sides of the bowl occasionally and breaking up any large lumps of sugar, for about 5 minutes, until thick and pale.

LUSCIOUS CHOCOLATE CUSTARD ICE CREAM

Serve this in stemmed glasses and top with a rich chocolate SAUCE (see chapter 8) or a splash of your favorite chocolate, coffee, or orange liqueur for a fancy dinner party, or dish it out in simple homey bowls for a family dinner. You'll love the caramel flavor from the brown sugar. **MAKES 1 QUART**

BRING the milk, cream, and salt just to a boil in a medium saucepan over medium-high heat. In a slow, steady stream, pour the milk mixture into the egg mixture, whisking constantly. Return the mixture to the saucepan and cook, whisking constantly, over low heat, for about 7 minutes, just until the whisk leaves definite trails in the custard. Remove from the heat and let cool for 10 minutes.

WHISK the chocolate into the custard in 2 batches, whisking until smooth after each addition. Whisk in the vanilla. Pour through a strainer set over a bowl, and let cool to room temperature.

REFRIGERATE, covered, until very cold, at least 3 hours; or quick-chill the mixture (see page 123).

TRANSFER the mixture to an ice cream maker and freeze according to the manufacturer's instructions. The ice cream will be soft when churned, but ready to eat. For a firmer texture, transfer to a freezer container and freeze for at least 2 hours. (This is best served the day it is made.)

SERVE scooped into bowls or stemmed glasses.

2 cups half-and-half

½ cup packed dark brown sugar

6 ounces bittersweet or
semisweet chocolate, finely chopped

One 8-ounce container
crème fraîche chilled

2 tablespoons light corn syrup

I teaspoon pure vanilla extract

Pinch of salt

BRING the half-and-half and sugar just to a boil in a medium saucepan over medium-high heat, whisking until the sugar is dissolved. Remove the pan from the heat, add the chocolate, and whisk until smooth. Transfer the mixture to a bowl and let cool to room temperature, whisking occasionally.

CHOCOLATE CRÈME FRAÎCHE ICE CREAM

I love this. The subtle tartness from the crème fraîche and the caramel flavor of the dark brown sugar make for a very rich, sweet, and tart flavor that I find irresistible. You need to be a bit careful when you're making an ice cream without eggs and a custard base; just pay attention to it at the end. If the churning goes on too long, the crème fraîche could turn to butter. Try this with chocolate sauce and/or with sliced ripe fruit or berries. **MAKES ABOUT I QUART**

REFRIGERATE, covered, until thoroughly chilled, about 2 hours; or quick-chill the mixture (see page 123).

WHISK together the crème fraîche, corn syrup, vanilla, and salt in a large bowl. Slowly add the chocolate mixture, whisking constantly until smooth.

TRANSFER the mixture to an ice cream maker and freeze according to the manufacturer's instructions. The ice cream will be soft when churned, but ready to eat. For a firmer texture, transfer to a freezer container, and freeze for at least 2 hours.

SERVE scooped into bowls or stemmed glasses

3 cups whole milk

6 large egg yolks

½ cup unsweetened cocoa powder

½ cup packed light brown sugar

½ cup light corn syrup

Pinch of salt

5 ounces bittersweet or semisweet chocolate, finely chopped

WHISK together ½ cup of the milk, the egg yolks, cocoa, sugar, corn syrup, and salt in a large bowl until smooth.

BITTERSWEET CHOCOLATE GELATO

Made in the Italian style, with milk rather than cream, this packs a tremendous amount of flavor. Intense chocolate for true chocolate lovers.

MAKES A GENEROUS 1 QUART

BRING the remaining 2½ cups milk just to a boil in a large saucepan over medium-high heat. In a slow, steady stream, pour the hot milk into the yolk mixture, whisking constantly. Return the mixture to the saucepan and cook over medium-low heat, whisking constantly, for 5 to 7 minutes, just until the whisk leaves definite trails in the custard. Remove the pan from the heat, add the chocolate, and whisk until smooth. Pour through a strainer set over a bowl. Let cool to room temperature.

REFRIGERATE, covered, until thoroughly chilled, about 3 hours; or quick-chill the mixture (see page 123).

TRANSFER the mixture to an ice cream maker and freeze according to the manufacturer's instructions. The gelato will be soft when churned, but ready to eat. For a firmer texture, transfer to a freezer container, and freeze for at least 2 hours.

SERVE scooped into bowls or stemmed glasses.

4 KATHARINE HEPBURN'S BROWNIES
(page 108) or 8 NIB NOUGATINE
BROWNIES (page 110)

2 cups LUSCIOUS CHOCOLATE
CUSTARD ICE CREAM (page 118) or
1 pint favorite store-bought vanilla ice cream

½ to ¾ cup SIMPLE HOT FUDGE SAUCE
(page 136), warmed

¼ cup CHERRY SAUCE (page 140)
or BLACKBERRY, STRAWBERRY, or
RASPBERRY SAUCE (page 138) (optional)

CHOCOLATE WHIPPED CREAM (page 141)

BROWNIE HOT FUDGE ICE CREAM SUNDAES

Adding a fruit sauce with the chocolate sauce to this brownie sundae would make it even better than remarkable. My favorites are CHERRY SAUCE and RASPBERRY SAUCE. If you'd rather, use plain sweetened whipped cream instead of the chocolate whipped cream: just whip 1 cup of cream to soft peaks with 1 to 2 tablespoons confectioners' sugar and ½ teaspoon pure vanilla extract.

SERVES 4

ARRANGE the brownies on 4 serving plates. Top with scoops of the ice cream and drizzle with the hot fudge sauce. Add a spoonful of the cherry sauce or a drizzle of the blackberry sauce, if using. Add a generous dollop of whipped cream to each sundae, and serve immediately.

2½ cups water

¾ cup packed light brown sugar

½ cup granulated sugar

⅔ cup unsweetened cocoa powder

Pinch of salt

4 ounces bittersweet or semisweet
chocolate, finely chopped

2 teaspoons pure vanilla extract

> **THE QUICK-CHILL METHOD** Simply put the ice cream mixture in a large glass measure or a deep bowl and place it in a shorter bowl. Add ice and water to the outer bowl and stir or whisk the ice cream mixture occasionally, adding more ice to the water as it melts, until the mixture is chilled. (Just make sure no ice gets in the mixture.)

CHOCOLATE SORBET

With its deep, rich chocolate flavor, this intense sorbet is superb served with slightly sweetened whipped cream, a very faint dusting of very finely ground chocolate nibs, or with cookies. Or as is. **MAKES 1 QUART**

BRING the water, brown sugar, granulated sugar, cocoa, and salt just to a boil in a medium heavy saucepan over medium-high heat, whisking until the sugar is dissolved. Remove the pan from the heat, add the chocolate, and whisk until smooth. Pour through a fine strainer set over a bowl and let cool to room temperature, then add the vanilla.

REFRIGERATE, covered, until thoroughly chilled, about 3 hours; or quick-chill the mixture (see above).

TRANSFER the mixture to an ice cream maker and freeze according to the manufacturer's instructions. The sorbet will be soft when churned, but ready to eat. For a firmer texture, transfer to a freezer container and freeze for at least 2 hours.

SERVE scooped into bowls or stemmed glasses.

7

No self-respecting chocolate cookbook would be complete without a few confections. It is possible that you might, on occasion, want to serve a dessert that isn't chocolate; but then, of course, you would need to serve something chocolate with the coffee and/or after-dinner drinks. For those instances, **LUSCIOUS HAZELNUT TRUFFLES** (page 126), **NIB TRUFFLES SQUARED** (page 131), **IRRESISTIBLE CHOCOLATE-PECAN CARAMELS** (page 128), or **CHOCOLATE-DIPPED STRAWBERRIES** (page 130) are just the thing. Any of these confections would also make a delightful extra or garnish for other desserts—a chocolate-dipped strawberry or a truffle on top of or on the side of just about any sweet is a lovely sight. And all of these confections are easy to make and grand to have on hand. Indulging in one during the afternoon can give you a reason to go on.

confections + a drink

NIB NOUGATINE (page 129), like a toffee made with cocoa nibs, is another terrific treat, as well as a great garnish. It's delicious to nibble on, but ground, crumbled, or even left in large shards it can offer an incomparable textural contrast to desserts plain and fancy. You'll find that **BICERIN** (page 133), an Italian chocolate and coffee drink from the seventeenth century, is a great, easy-to-prepare addition to your repertoire that will impress and delight your guests.

BRING the cream and salt just to a boil in a medium saucepan over medium heat. Remove the pan from the heat, add the chocolate, and whisk until smooth. Pour the mixture into a bowl and let cool to room temperature, then refrigerate, covered, for 2 to 3 hours, until firm.

MEANWHILE, preheat the oven to 350°F.

TOAST the hazelnuts on a baking sheet for 10 to 15 minutes, or until dark golden brown. Let cool completely, then finely chop and place in a shallow bowl.

1¼ cups heavy (whipping) cream

Pinch of salt

12 ounces bittersweet or semisweet chocolate, finely chopped

I cup hazelnut pieces

¼ cup unsweetened cocoa powder

LUSCIOUS HAZELNUT TRUFFLES

It used to be difficult to find hazelnuts but now, thankfully, they are packaged by Blue Diamond and available in supermarkets. The longer they are toasted, the sweeter they will be, and the better foil for bittersweet chocolate. There's nothing difficult about these truffles. They are supposed to be irregularly shaped; their roughness is part of their charm. And when you chop the hazelnuts, they will be different sizes, but that's part of the charm of the truffles as well. If you'd like, coat only half of the truffles with the cocoa—the two types look beautiful together.

MAKES 5 DOZEN TRUFFLES

PLACE the cocoa in another shallow bowl. Working quickly, roll a rounded measuring teaspoon of the chocolate mixture into a I-inch ball in your hands, then roll in the hazelnuts, pressing them lightly into the truffle, lightly coat with the cocoa, and set on a tray. Repeat with the remaining truffle mixture, hazelnuts, and cocoa.

STORE between layers of wax paper in an airtight container in the refrigerator until ready to serve, or for up to I week. Let the truffles stand at room temperature for about 15 minutes before serving.

NOTE: This is a very flexible recipe. Use any nut you'd like instead of hazelnuts, or coat the truffles with something else entirely—large clear sugar crystals, finely crushed graham crackers, or crushed hard peppermint candies would all be terrific. Or just use the cocoa, without nuts. Add a tablespoon or so of your favorite liqueur to the chocolate ganache, or use Cognac or other brandy or rum. If it pleases you, add instant espresso powder or replace some of the cream with mascarpone. You could also add minced dried tart cherries, a pinch of cinnamon or nutmeg, finely chopped fresh lemon or orange zest, or minced crystallized ginger. You can even steep Earl Gray tea, spices such as saffron or cardamom, or herbs (try rosemary or lemon verbena) in the cream to flavor it; strain and reheat gently before adding the chocolate.

2 cups sugar

1 cup heavy (whipping) cream

¾ cup sweetened condensed milk

1 cup light corn syrup

½ cup (1 stick) unsalted butter, cut into small pieces

1 cup toasted pecans, coarsely chopped

1 teaspoon pure vanilla extract

6 ounces bittersweet or semisweet chocolate, finely chopped

LINE a 9-inch square baking pan with foil, keeping the foil as smooth as possible. Butter the foil.

BRING the sugar, cream, condensed milk, corn syrup, and butter to a boil over medium heat in a large heavy nonstick saucepan, stirring until the sugar is dissolved. Increase the heat to medium-high and boil, without stirring, for about 15 minutes, or until the temperature reaches 246°F on a candy thermometer, washing down the sides of the pan with a damp pastry brush if you see any sugar crystals forming.

IRRESISTIBLE CHOCOLATE-PECAN CARAMELS

Adapted by Rosanne Toroian, cook extraordinaire, from a recipe in Lou Siebert Pappas' *The Christmas Candy Book*, and given to me, these buttery caramels are impossible to stop eating. They have the perfect ratio of caramel to chocolate, and those fabulous toasted pecans. Bet you'll love them, too. **MAKES 64 CARAMELS**

REMOVE the saucepan from the heat and stir in the pecans and vanilla. Pour the caramel mixture into the prepared pan and spread evenly (do not scrape out the saucepan; the caramel on the sides may contain sugar crystals). Sprinkle the chocolate over the hot caramel and let stand until it melts. Spread the chocolate with a rubber spatula to cover the caramel evenly. Let cool to room temperature, then refrigerate until the caramel is firm and the chocolate is set, 1 to 2 hours.

INVERT the pan onto an oiled cutting board, lift off the pan, and discard the foil. Cut the caramel into 8 strips, then cut each strip crosswise into 8 squares.

STORE the squares layered between wax paper in a tightly covered container. (The caramels will keep for up to 3 days at room temperature, 2 weeks in the refrigerator, and 1 month in the freezer.)

GENEROUSLY butter a 9-inch square baking pan. Sprinkle the cocoa nibs evenly in the pan.

⅓ cup cocoa nibs

¾ cup sugar

⅓ cup water

¼ cup light corn syrup

Pinch of salt

HEAT the sugar, water, corn syrup, and salt in a small heavy saucepan over medium heat, stirring, until the sugar is dissolved. Increase the heat to high and bring to a boil, washing down the sides of the pan with a damp pastry brush if you see any sugar crystals forming. Boil, without stirring, until the sugar mixture turns a dark golden brown—it should register 320° to 330°F on a candy thermometer—continuing to wash down the sides of the pan with a damp pastry brush if necessary.

NIB NOUGATINE

Use a Polder candy thermometer (see sidebar) or judge the doneness of the nougatine by the color. Just cook the sugar mixture until it reaches a dark brown but is not burned. (You might want to use a thermometer the first couple of times you make it, just to be sure.) Use the nougatine broken into large chunks or shards or into small pieces, or crush it in a food processor for a very handy powder for garnishing just about anything. This nougatine is a bit like peanut brittle, with the peanuts replaced by cocoa nibs. **MAKES ABOUT 8 OUNCES**

IMMEDIATELY remove the saucepan from the heat and carefully pour the caramel over the nibs: try pouring it in even parallel lines and then carefully and gently shake the pan to distribute it as evenly as possible. Let the nougatine cool in the pan on a wire rack until set.

BREAK the nougatine into pieces, or transfer to a plastic bag and crush with a rolling pin. Or pulse in a food processor to ¼-inch pieces; then, if desired, continue to process until the praline is pulverized to a powder.

CANDY THERMOMETERS I love making candy, but I can't stand those old-fashioned candy thermometers. Ungainly and awkward, often they can't even reach low enough in the pan to register small amounts. Using a Polder probe thermometer, which has both a probe that fits easily into any container and an alarm for when your food hits the temperature you're looking for, totally changed my attitude. When making the IRRESISTIBLE CHOCOLATE-PECAN CARAMELS (facing page) or the NIB NOUGATINE you can set the alarm to go off when the sugar mixture reaches the right temperature.

3 ounces bittersweet or
semisweet chocolate, chopped

2 teaspoons flavorless vegetable oil

1 pint ripe medium strawberries

CHOCOLATE-DIPPED STRAWBERRIES

You can dip almost any fruit in this way, whether fresh, glazed, or dried. Crystallized ginger is fabulous, too. And an assortment (like fresh strawberries, crystallized ginger, and dried apricots) is especially brilliant. But the fruit you dip must be dry. If you use dried fruit instead of the strawberries, you'll need about 4 ounces total for the 3 ounces of chocolate. **SERVES 4 TO 6**

MELT the chocolate with the oil in a small deep heatproof bowl set over a saucepan of about 1½ inches of nearly simmering water, whisking until smooth. Remove the bowl from the heat.

LINE a baking sheet with wax paper. Dip each strawberry into the chocolate, covering about two-thirds of it and turning to coat evenly, then shake off any excess and carefully place on the wax paper. Tilt the bowl as necessary to make coating the berries easier, and if the chocolate begins to cool, return the bowl briefly to the saucepan to heat it.

LET the berries stand for about 30 minutes, until the chocolate is set. Carefully remove the berries from the wax paper.

SERVE immediately, or refrigerate for up to 8 hours before serving.

LIGHTLY oil an 8-inch square baking pan and line the bottom with parchment or wax paper.

MELT 12 ounces of the chocolate with the cream in a heatproof bowl set over a saucepan of about 1½ inches of nearly simmering water, whisking until smooth. Remove the pan from the heat, add the vanilla and salt, and whisk until smooth. Set aside.

I pound bittersweet or semisweet chocolate, chopped

¾ cup heavy (whipping) cream

½ teaspoon pure vanilla extract

Pinch of salt

⅓ cup cocoa nibs

MELT the remaining 4 ounces chocolate in another heatproof bowl set over the same saucepan of nearly simmering water, whisking until smooth. Pour half of this chocolate into the prepared pan and spread with a rubber spatula to coat the bottom evenly. Refrigerate for about 5 minutes to set the chocolate.

NIB TRUFFLES SQUARED

Sleek truffle squares or rectangles seem more sophisticated than the traditional rounds. These are especially elegant— and the very essence of chocolate. Instead of the nibs, try topping the truffles with coarsely chopped green pistachios, toasted sliced almonds, or even *matcha* (powdered ceremonial green tea). You might also replace ¼ cup of the cream with a liqueur—crème de cassis is particularly good.

MAKES **64** SQUARE TRUFFLES OR **32** RECTANGULAR TRUFFLES

SPREAD the chocolate and cream mixture over the set chocolate. Sprinkle the nibs evenly over the top and gently press them into the chocolate. Using a fork, drizzle the remaining melted chocolate over the top. Let cool to room temperature, then refrigerate, covered, until very firm, 3 to 4 hours, or as long as overnight.

RUN a table knife around the edges of the pan. Turn the truffle mixture out onto a cutting board and peel away the parchment paper. Let stand for 5 minutes, for easier cutting. With a sharp knife, cut the truffles into 8 strips and then cut each strip into 8 squares, or cut into 4 strips and then cut each strip into 8 rectangles.

STORE in the refrigerator in an airtight container between layers of wax paper until ready to serve, or for up to 2 weeks. Let stand at room temperature for a few minutes before serving.

2 cups whole milk

2 cups hot strong brewed coffee

3 ounces bittersweet or
semisweet chocolate, finely chopped

3 tablespoons sugar, or to taste

BICERIN

Drink your dessert! Pronounced "beech-en-REEN," *bicerin* was a favorite drink of café society in Turin, Italy, in the 1600s, and it is still enjoyed there today. I've adapted this recipe from one in *A Passion for Piedmont* by Matt Kramer. If you like, you can add a quarter-teaspoon or so of orange-flower water for an authentic, aromatic, and very floral touch. **SERVES 4 TO 6**

BRING the milk just to a boil in a medium saucepan over medium heat.

MEANWHILE, pour the coffee into a heatproof pitcher or glass measure and whisk in the chocolate and sugar until smooth. Whisk in the hot milk. Taste and add more sugar, if desired.

There is nothing like chocolate ice cream and hot fudge sauce, no better combination of textures. But you don't need to spend a lot of time making hot fudge sauce: try my **SIMPLE HOT FUDGE SAUCE** (page 136), made in minutes. You simply can't have too many chocolate sauces in your repertoire, so I've included two creamy chocolate sauces, one prepared with heavy cream and one with crème fraîche, which is stupendous combined with chocolate. You can make **DEEP DARK CHOCOLATE OR MOCHA SAUCE** (page 137) by using either water or brewed coffee as the liquid of choice in the recipe. And last, but not at all least, there's a **CHOCOLATE CARAMEL SAUCE** (page 139) that would be good on just about anything. Try adding crushed **NIB NOUGATINE** (page 129) to any of these chocolate sauces—it's bliss.

sauces

Fruit is brilliant with chocolate. My favorite combination is cherries and chocolate and I recommend either the **CHOCOLATE CHERRY SAUCE** (page 138) or the **CHERRY SAUCE** (page 140). Make sure to try **BLACKBERRY, STRAWBERRY, OR RASPBERRY SAUCE** (page 138) with your favorite chocolate desserts. When you need a chocolate syrup, say for an ice cream soda or to drizzle over just about any chocolate treat, make the deeply flavored **CHOCOLATE SYRUP** (page 140). If you like whipped cream, you'll love the **CHOCOLATE WHIPPED CREAM** (page 141) over any dessert, chocolate or not, and whenever you would use plain ol' whipped cream. Then there's the **CHOCOLATE-BALSAMIC DRIZZLE** (page 141)—don't knock it until you've tried it. I have a friend who uses it on grilled vegetables! If it's good on grilled zucchini, imagine how good it will be on **LUSCIOUS CHOCOLATE CUSTARD ICE CREAM** (page 118).

1 cup heavy (whipping) cream

2 tablespoons light corn syrup

Pinch of salt

8 ounces bittersweet or
semisweet chocolate, finely chopped

SIMPLE HOT FUDGE SAUCE

Quick and easy, as well as foolproof.
Make up a batch of this and keep it in
your refrigerator for emergencies.
(You may find you have one every day.)

MAKES 1½ CUPS

BRING the cream, corn syrup, and salt just to a boil in a medium heavy saucepan over medium-high heat, whisking until smooth. Remove the pan from the heat, add the chocolate, and whisk until smooth.

USE immediately, or let cool to room temperature, transfer to a glass jar, and refrigerate, tightly covered, until ready to use. (The sauce will keep for up to 2 months.) Gently reheat before serving.

12 ounces bittersweet or
semisweet chocolate, finely chopped, or
one 12-ounce bag semisweet chocolate chips

½ cup heavy (whipping) cream

6 tablespoons water

Pinch of salt

CREAMY CHOCOLATE SAUCE

This is a CHOCOLATE SAUCE, not a
chocolate sauce. It makes a
generous amount, but if you store it in
a glass jar, you can just heat the
sauce in the jar in a saucepan of
warm water—no muss, no fuss.

MAKES 2 CUPS

MELT the chocolate with the cream, water, and salt in a heatproof bowl set over a saucepan of about 1½ inches of nearly simmering water, whisking until smooth.

USE immediately, or let cool to room temperature, transfer to a glass jar, and refrigerate, tightly covered, until ready to use. (The sauce will keep for up to 2 months.) Gently reheat before serving.

One 8-ounce container crème fraîche

8 ounces bittersweet or
semisweet chocolate, finely chopped

Pinch of salt

CHOCOLATE
CRÈME FRAÎCHE SAUCE

The crème fraîche gives this sauce
a fabulous smooth consistency
and a lovely little tang that is very
sophisticated and urbane.

MAKES 1¾ CUPS

HEAT the crème fraîche in a medium saucepan over very low heat until liquid. Add the chocolate and salt and whisk until smooth.

USE immediately, or let cool to room temperature, transfer to a glass jar, and refrigerate, tightly covered, until ready to use. (The sauce will keep for up to 2 months.) Gently reheat before serving.

8 ounces bittersweet
or semisweet chocolate, finely chopped

¾ to 1 cup water or brewed coffee

Pinch of salt

DEEP DARK CHOCOLATE
OR MOCHA SAUCE

A sauce with pure unadulterated chocolate
flavor, enhanced with the flavor of
coffee if you like, this is very handy to have
around. Depending on how thick or thin
you want the sauce to be, use more or less
water or coffee.

MAKES ABOUT 2 CUPS

MELT the chocolate with the water and salt in a heat-proof bowl set over a saucepan of about 1½ inches of nearly simmering water, whisking until smooth.

USE immediately, or let cool to room temperature, transfer to a glass jar, and refrigerate, tightly covered, until ready to use. (The sauce will keep for up to 2 months.) Shake well before serving chilled, or gently reheat before serving.

1 cup heavy (whipping) cream

¾ cup pitted ripe cherries, finely chopped

4 ounces bittersweet or
semisweet chocolate, finely chopped

Pinch of salt

CHOCOLATE CHERRY SAUCE

*My favorite fruit with chocolate is
cherries, but you could use fresh
or thawed frozen berries or other chopped
fruit, such as peaches, instead.*

MAKES 1½ CUPS

HEAT the cream, cherries, chocolate, and salt in a medium heavy saucepan over low heat, stirring, until the chocolate is melted. Remove from the heat and let stand for 10 minutes.

POUR the mixture through a large coarse strainer set over a bowl, pressing hard on the solids to extract as much liquid as possible.

USE immediately, or let cool to room temperature, transfer to a glass jar, and refrigerate, tightly covered, until ready to serve. (The sauce will keep for up to 2 weeks.) Shake well before serving chilled, or gently reheat before serving.

3 cups fresh blackberries, strawberries,
or raspberries

½ to ¾ cup confectioners' sugar
(depending on the sweetness of the berries)

2 tablespoons water

1 to 2 teaspoons fresh lemon juice

BLACKBERRY, STRAWBERRY, OR RASPBERRY SAUCE

*Pulse the berries just until pureed; the
longer they are processed, the more likely
you are to break open the seeds, and they
might release a slightly bitter flavor.*

MAKES A SCANT 2 CUPS

PUREE the berries in a food processor. Sift the sugar over the berries, add the water, and pulse until smooth.

POUR the mixture through a large coarse strainer set over a bowl, pressing hard on the solids to extract as much liquid as possible. Stir in the lemon juice to taste.

TRANSFER to a glass jar and refrigerate, tightly covered, until ready to serve. (The sauce will keep for up to 1 week.) Shake well before serving the sauce chilled or at room temperature. The sauce will thicken a bit on standing; add water as needed to thin to the desired consistency before serving.

4 ounces bittersweet
or semisweet chocolate, finely chopped

1 cup warm water

Pinch of salt

1 cup heavy (whipping) cream

2 cups sugar

2 tablespoons light corn syrup

CHOCOLATE CARAMEL SAUCE

There is nothing complicated about making caramel, but it is one of those things that you need to do in order to really get a sense of it. I'm not saying it won't be perfect the first time you make it, just that if you're feeling a little tentative, you'll become very confident after you've made a batch or two.

Watch the syrup carefully, swirling it occasionally until the syrup is a dark caramel color. Do not let the syrup get too dark, or it will be bitter, but if the caramel is too light, the sauce will be too sweet. It is easiest to judge the color if you drip a few drops onto a white plate. And don't use a saucepan with a dark bottom, or it'll be too difficult to see the color of the caramel.

MAKES 2 CUPS

MELT the chocolate with ¼ cup of the water and the salt in a heatproof bowl set over a saucepan of simmering water, whisking until smooth. Meanwhile, heat the cream in a small saucepan over medium heat just until hot. Set both aside, covered, to keep warm.

HEAT the sugar, the remaining ¾ cup water, and the corn syrup in a large heavy saucepan over medium heat, stirring, until the sugar is dissolved. Increase the heat to high and bring to a boil, washing down the sides of the pan with a damp pastry brush if you see any sugar crystals forming. Boil, without stirring, until the caramel turns a dark golden brown, continuing to wash down the sides of the pan occasionally if necessary.

IMMEDIATELY remove the saucepan from the heat. Being careful to avoid the spatters, stir in the warm cream about 2 tablespoons at a time. Return the pan to low heat and cook, whisking, until the sauce is smooth. Remove the pan from the heat, add the chocolate mixture, and whisk until smooth.

USE immediately, or let cool to room temperature, transfer to a glass jar, and refrigerate, tightly covered, until ready to serve. (The sauce will keep for up to 2 months.) Gently reheat the sauce before serving, adding a little water or cream if necessary to thin slightly.

I tablespoon unsalted butter
or flavorless vegetable oil

2 cups (12 ounces) ripe Bing cherries, pitted

2 to 3 tablespoons light brown sugar

Pinch of salt

CHERRY SAUCE

Use ripe Bing cherries, and serve this
with just about anything chocolate.
If you want to serve the sauce chilled or
at room temperature, use the vegetable
oil rather than the butter.

MAKES ABOUT 1½ CUPS

MELT the butter in a medium nonstick skillet over medium heat. Add the cherries and cook, stirring frequently, for 3 to 5 minutes, until they begin to release their juices. Add the sugar and salt, increase the heat to high, and bring to a boil. Reduce the heat to low and simmer, stirring, for 4 minutes, or until the sugar has dissolved and the juices have thickened slightly.

REMOVE the skillet from the heat.

COOL slightly and serve, or cool to room temperature, transfer to a glass jar, and refrigerate, tightly covered, until ready to serve. (The sauce will keep for up to 2 days.) Reheat gently before serving, or serve chilled or at room temperature.

2 cups water

½ cup unsweetened cocoa powder

I cup packed dark brown sugar

4 ounces bittersweet or
semisweet chocolate, finely chopped

¼ cup light corn syrup

¼ teaspoon salt

1½ teaspoons pure vanilla extract

CHOCOLATE SYRUP

You'll be happy to have this on hand.
There's very little it wouldn't improve.

MAKES 3½ CUPS

WHISK together the water and cocoa in a large heavy saucepan until almost smooth. Bring to a boil over medium-high heat. Add the sugar, chocolate, corn syrup, and salt and cook, whisking, until the sugar is dissolved. Reduce the heat to low and simmer for 5 minutes.

LET the syrup cool to room temperature, and stir in the vanilla.

USE immediately, or transfer to a glass jar and refrigerate, tightly covered, until ready to use. (The syrup will keep for several months.) Shake well before serving chilled, or gently reheat before serving.

1 cup heavy (whipping) cream

¼ cup chilled CHOCOLATE SYRUP (facing page)
or store-bought chocolate syrup

CHOCOLATE WHIPPED CREAM

If you would rather prepare this
with unsweetened cocoa powder than
chocolate syrup, add about 4 to 6 tablespoons
of confectioners' sugar and sift in 3 to 4
tablespoons unsweetened cocoa, to taste.
You could also try 5 to 6 tablespoons
of chocolate-flavored malted milk powder
instead of the syrup, or 1 to 2 tablespoons
along with the syrup, adjusting the
sugar to taste.

MAKES ABOUT 2 CUPS

BEAT the cream with an electric mixer on medium-high speed in a large deep bowl just until it begins to thicken. Add the chocolate syrup and beat just until the cream forms soft peaks when the beaters are lifted.

USE immediately, or cover tightly and refrigerate for up to 4 hours.

¾ cup packed light brown sugar

½ cup balsamic vinegar

1½ ounces bittersweet
or semisweet chocolate, finely chopped

CHOCOLATE-BALSAMIC DRIZZLE

This is fun, and really different!
Inspired by a recipe in Chantal Coady's
Real Chocolate, it's ideal as a topping for
fruit, berries, ice cream, or whatever you
dream up. It's a little puckery, so you don't
need much, just a squiggle or a drizzle.
And don't splurge with your best artisanal
balsamic here—use a commercial one.

MAKES A SCANT 1 CUP

BRING the sugar and vinegar just to a boil in a small saucepan over medium-high heat, whisking until the sugar is dissolved. Reduce the heat and simmer for 3 minutes. Remove the pan from the heat, add the chocolate, and whisk until smooth.

USE immediately, or cool to room temperature, transfer to a glass jar, and refrigerate, tightly covered, until ready to use. (The drizzle will keep for up to 2 weeks.) Serve at room temperature or warm, shaking the jar or gently reheating before serving.

INDEX

TABLE OF EQUIVALENTS

The exact equivalents in the following tables have been rounded for convenience.

LIQUID / DRY MEASURES

U.S.	METRIC
1/4 teaspoon	1.25 milliliters
1/2 teaspoon	2.5 milliliters
1 teaspoon	5 milliliters
1 tablespoon (3 teaspoons)	15 milliliters
1 fluid ounce (2 tablespoons)	30 milliliters
1/4 cup	60 milliliters
1/3 cup	80 milliliters
1/2 cup	120 milliliters
1 cup	240 milliliters
1 pint (2 cups)	480 milliliters
1 quart (4 cups, 32 ounces)	960 milliliters
1 gallon (4 quarts)	3.84 liters
1 ounce (by weight)	28 grams
1 pound	454 grams
2.2 pounds	1 kilogram

LENGTH

U.S.	METRIC
1/8 inch	3 millimeters
1/4 inch	6 millimeters
1/2 inch	12 millimeters
1 inch	2.5 centimeters

OVEN TEMPERATURE

FAHRENHEIT	CELSIUS	GAS
250	120	1/2
275	140	1
300	150	2
325	160	3
350	180	4
375	190	5
400	200	6
425	220	7
450	230	8
475	240	9
500	260	10